ALPHABETICAL BRITAIN

Travelling Around Britain By Train

Andy Keen

KDPublishing

To Catherine

FOREWORD

The maps provided at the start of most chapters are schematic and not to scale nor do they show every station or line. Nevertheless I hope you find them useful.

THE PLAN

Several years ago, my friend Kristyan travelled round our home city of Stoke-on-Trent by bus from A to Z. He started in Abbey Hulton and ended in Zodiac Drive.

No reason, just a bit of fun. And why not. He had a travelling companion or two, and someone who met them, by car, in various places during the day to offer sustenance.

But he basically spent the day on buses travelling the city. He wasn't even homeless. Abbey Hulton, Baddely Green, Chell...on he went. Eventually ending up on a late bus in Zodiac Drive.

I had thought of doing the city numerically by bus. Route 1 then 2 and so on. But this was considerably more complex as bus routes do not always, or indeed often, tie up with each other numerically. And I fancied a bigger challenge.

My plan was to do Britain alphabetically by train. I would start at a station beginning with A, travel to a station beginning with B travel to a station beginning with C and so on. There are no stations beginning with X or Z, it is almost like they did not have this challenge in mind when naming stations, so just twenty-four stations in total.

Put like that, it did not sound too bad at all. Just twenty-four stations, in alphabetical order. How hard can it be?

The devil, as they say, was in the detail. I needed rules. I was going to do this properly or not at all. You must have rules, otherwise there would be anarchy.

The planning was crucial, there are few stations starting with a Q for example, so I would need one that was near a P and an R. So, I would then have to ensure the P was near an O. It was all getting complex.

There are only four stations starting with J, and only twenty-three starting I, so finding an I and J on the same line would be a problem. Even Y produces fifteen names, and the preceding W a massive two hundred and four. At least ending should not be too hard then.

There are stations I would love to include in this challenge, for one reason or another, but they simply are not practical. Take poor Newhaven Marine for example. Officially it is still open (at time of writing,) and a train still runs there-just one a day-but no passengers are allowed on it, and you can't buy a ticket to or from Newhaven Marine station anymore. The train is not even shown in public timetables. There is no way it could be my N station, not when there are another eighty-seven with a useable service. But I wanted to go. Where these stations occur, they get their own entry under that letter, but are not part of the journey. They are just a bonus.

THE RULES

I did not want to make it unnecessarily complicated. It was already pointless, no need to be complicated too. But equally, there needed to be some rules, otherwise it was just a pointless journey without purpose. At least this way it was a pointless journey with a purpose.

I would travel from one station to the next on a direct train, only if this were not possible (usually because one of the more obscure letters of the alphabet was involved) would a change of train be permitted.

The letters X and Z were to be ignored. This was not an A-Z journey, but an A-W + Y journey. There are simply no stations at all starting with X or Z. And trying to pretend "Kings Cross" would do for X, as it is a cross, did not seem like an argument to me.

Which brings me to my next point. The official station name, that is the one on the platform name boards, must begin with the required letter. So, "Euston" station is an L station, as the name boards read "London Euston."

Only National Rail stations qualify. That is, stations that are served by National Rail trains. So, London Underground stations are out, as are heritage or steam railway stations, unless National Rail services call there too. And the trains must be in the timetable, no special trains allowed. Once again, Newhaven Marine is disqualified.

It would be permissible to alight at a station starting with a letter and continue from a different station starting with the same letter, as long as I travelled between the two using only my own two legs. This, of course, allowed for places with more than one station on different lines. I could, for example, arrive at Blackpool South for my B, walk along the seafront to Blackpool North and get on a train there to get to C. But I could not travel between the two Blackpool stations by tram, bus or horse-drawn carriage.

Armed with these rules, I was ready to set off. But where to choose for A? There were one hundred and twenty-six jostling contenders. But I knew my choice.

Kidsgrove

ALSAGER

Stoke-On-Trent

BARLASTON

Stone

NORTON BRIDGE

BIRMINGHAM
NEW STREET

BIRMINGHAM SNOW HILL

BIRMINGHAM MOOR STREET

BORDESLEY

A

When I was six months old, we moved to Alsager, in Cheshire, where I stayed till I was Twenty-Four. We did not have a car, so we travelled by train a lot. All our journeys started and ended at Alsager as we could walk from our house.

To start my modern-day journey, it seemed as good a starting point as any. And better than many.

Alsager station was opened in 1848 and is around half a mile from the town centre. When built, it had a station masters house, toilets, waiting rooms, a ticket office and a full complement of porters to look after your needs. Now, more people use it, so it has less facilities. There are just brick built shelters on both platforms, only one of which has windows so you can actually see the train coming.

The station masters house is still standing but is now a private residence and not connected with the railway. All the other original buildings have been demolished after many years of standing empty and rotting away.

When I was a child there was a signal box. It also worked the road level crossing gate. If the train was late, the signalman would lean out of the window and shout across the road "Crewe train ten minutes late" or whatever.

Then, in 1985, they closed and demolished the signal box, and operated the level crossing barriers, by camera, remotely from Crewe.

At the same time, they installed loudspeakers on the platform, these too were connected to Crewe and gave announcements about trains at Alsager for the first time ever. They did not last long as the neighbouring houses complained about them. Silence, and lack of travel information, reigned supreme for a few years; before they installed visual displays and much quieter auto-mated announcements.

Automated announcements are probably an improvement on no announcements, but they do not pronounce Alsager correctly!

No one is quite sure where the name Alsager comes from. It is recorded in the Doomsday book (as Eleacier) but from there, for-ward or backward, history is a bit vague.

If you arrive into Alsager by car, you are greeted by signs telling you it is a "Fairtrade Town". Whatever that means. Those arriving by train are not provided with this information. Presumably, cars are fairer than trains.

There is a plaque on the council offices wall proudly proclaiming Alsager won "Village Of The Year" in 1985. There is no mention of what has happened since then.

I stood on the station platform now, waiting. The display boards saying the train was on time, this looked like a good start. A couple of minutes before it was due, the barriers went down to close the road to traffic.

The train trundled into view and rolled into the platform. I got on and we set off bang on time. The automated announcement kicked in "Welcome aboard this London NorthWestern Railway service to Birmingham New Street."

The next stop was Kidsgrove, here the line from Crewe joins the main line from London to Manchester. My train picked up speed and sped through Longport, it being decided that the people there do not need to go to Birmingham and the hourly Derby trains meet their needs.

The next stop is Stoke on Trent. The minutes we saved by not calling at Longport are sat here instead. It makes sense to someone.

Then we continue down the main line, before veering off again at Stone. There used to be four platforms here. Two on the London lines, and two where we were now, on the Birmingham lines. British Rail decided, in their infinite wisdom, that the people of Stone don't want to go to London and removed those ones in the 1940's.

Stone station suffered a further indignity in 1993 when the ticket office was closed, and the station staff removed. In 2003 the train service was "temporarily suspended" during the West Coast mainline upgrade. Only management realised they then had a spare train and used it on other routes, when the upgrade work was completed the service never restarted. It took until 2008, a full five years of "temporary", before trains resumed.

After Penkridge we avoid the direct route into Birmingham as we have to serve Wolverhampton. There used to be a First-Class Lounge here, but then it was decided the people of Wolverhampton do not deserve these kinds of things, and it shut.

The route between Wolverhampton and Birmingham is very busy. Not just trains, but also buses and trams ply between the two. Birmingham having all the attractions, Wolverhampton having the houses. It matters not what day of the week or the time of day you travel, your train between Wolverhampton and Birmingham will be full. Mine was no exception.

You know you are arriving into Birmingham New Street as you go into a tunnel, it does not matter which way you arrive into Birmingham from, you will be in a tunnel. It really is the most dismal of welcomes.

The automated announcements kick-in "We are now approaching Birmingham New Street" some people get up and get ready, the regulars wait. They know we will stop in the tunnel before the station. Train drivers apparently nickname it 'The Crucible'; as you have to get a red before you can get a colour.

After our darkened wait in the tunnel, we move into the station. I can tick another letter off on my alphabetical challenge.

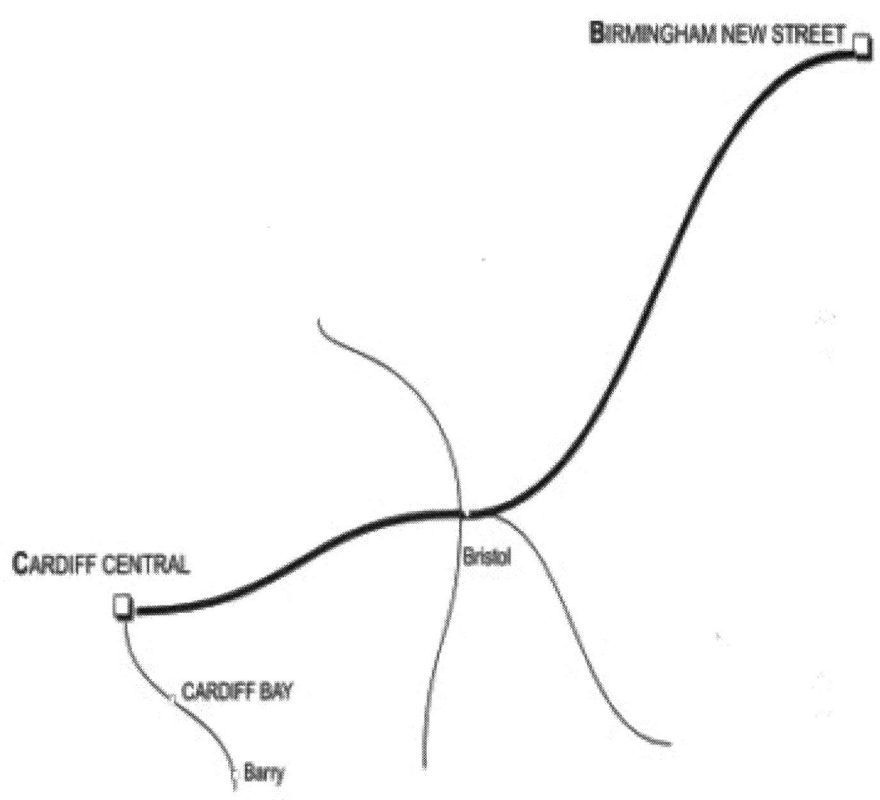

B

Birmingham New Street is, according to Network Rail who own all of Britain's stations, the busiest station outside of London. It also has the largest number of platforms, with 25. But do not go expecting to catch a train from platform 25.

The station is a confusing layout whichever way you look at it. The twenty-five platforms are numbered 1-12, so straight away it is not simple. Each platform is divided into 'A' and 'B' ends, so it is numbered from platform 1A to 12B. The mathematical amongst you will have noted that twelve times two is twenty-four. Platform 4 also has a small dead-end platform, numbered, with breath-taking originality, 4C.

In effect, each platform (apart from 4C) can be used as three. A train can, for example, arrive and depart from platform 1A, whilst another simultaneously does the same in 1B. But only small trains. Anything over five coaches, and it needs to use both the 'A' and 'B' platforms, which is called 'Platform 1'.

They do not keep figures for the number of people who get on the wrong train at Birmingham, but I am guessing it is quite high. Possibly higher than the people who get on the right train.

Birmingham New Street is just one of three city centre stations with the name Birmingham in them. It is the darkest and most bleak, although Birmingham Snow Hill gives it a good go too.

New Street station sits underneath a shopping centre. If you wander to the platform extremities it is possible to see daylight, but you are still low down, and walls tower up all around you. It gives the impression of being in a pit.

In recent years, the shopping centre has been rebuilt, and it is rather pleasant. But the station remains dark and damp, and with train diesel fumes filling the air. At shopping centre level, there is a glass dome roof letting in a lot of natural light, but there is nowhere for this to filter down to the platforms, and there is nowhere to sit in this area to wait.

They do have waiting rooms. They are called, red, blue and yellow waiting rooms. Although you never know which you are in, as they are all grey. There is also a First-Class Lounge for First Class ticket holders. Or at least some First-Class ticket holders. Because train companies do not like to work together for the passengers' benefit, only people who have a First-Class ticket with the providers of the Lounge can use it. No one else with a First-Class ticket can.

With time to kill, I had a look around Birmingham's other stations. New Street station is a short walk away from both Snow Hill and Moor Street. When you come out of New Street station, the first surprise is to find you are not on New Street, the station is actually on Stephenson Street, New Street is the next road up. I would like to say it is historical and the entrance moved, but it has never had an entrance onto New Street.

Birmingham Snow Hill is a station with only local services, it is, really, a commuter station. However, it too is in a basement, although under offices rather than a shopping centre. But it manages the same dark, dank feeling of New Street station, but with more diesel fumes as it is not electrified. The train journey from Snow Hill to Moor Street is entirely in a tunnel.

Birmingham Moor Street station on the other hand, is a delight and a pleasure. It is light, bright and airy, a pleasure to wait for trains. It has been restored as if it were the 1930's, but with modern facilities and no air raids.

In the 1980's Moor Street station was in a poor way. It closed-sort of-in 1987, with services moved from the original terminus station to a new through station next door. Services were extended through to a newly reopened Snow Hill station. The Moor Street terminus was left to rot away and fall into disrepair. Not helped by a runaway bus crashing into the buildings.

Then a change in its fortunes with a rise in passenger numbers, the tunnel between Snow Hill and Moor Street could not cope with demand, so more services were introduced from Moor Street, requiring the return of the terminus station. It was fully modernised, whilst keeping its 1930's charm.

The station was returned to its former glory in 2003, the platforms were wonderful, the waiting rooms delightful, the toilets spotless. It was just a shame that Network Rail did not connect the track to start being able to run trains until 2010. Even then, they only reconnected two of the three platforms. The third has not been connected even now.

Back at New Street station and it was time to board my train to Cardiff Central. But I was not done with Birmingham completely. There is another B that I went back too. Bordesley.

Bordesley is unusual. In the timetable it has just one train a week, in one direction only. Yet just under 21,000 people a year use the station! I could not let the opportunity pass me by.

The weekly train is on a Saturday and heads into Birmingham. With just the one train, I could not arrive and depart by train. At least, not without spending a week there, so I walked to the station.

The line from Moor Street station is raised up on a viaduct so is easy to follow, I followed the main road running parallel to the line. I then turned off to follow a road under the railway. Strangely, under this bridge, is a bus stop. With a shelter. Why they felt the need to put a shelter under a bridge I cannot begin to imagine.

Behind this was the entrance to Bordesley station. As entrances go, it is not the most welcoming. There is a secure metal grill fencing just to add to the sense of foreboding. However, the gate was open. Someone drives out in a van each Saturday morning to unlock it, and every Saturday afternoon to lock it again. It is not worth them hanging around to sell tickets.

Through the gate and a dark staircase awaits. I climbed up and arrived onto platform level. There is a brick waiting shelter, which is only open one side, but as trains only come one way it does not matter. It is just a shame the side that permits waiting is not the same side that the train comes.

I was a little early, as the walk had not taken as long as I thought it might. So I stood on this bleak platform, there are no seats, waiting for the train. Several other trains passed; the drivers seemingly surprised to see anyone there. The high passenger numbers for the station are because of its close proximity to Birmingham City Football Stadium. They stop extra trains on home match days. Most Saturdays no one gets on or off.

Eventually, my train came into view. The driver remembered to stop, the guard opened the doors and was surprised to find someone wanting to get on. No one got off.

With that, the train set off and was back at Birmingham Moor Street in minutes, only quicker. Bordesley is not the only unusual B though.

Unbelievably, Barlaston has an even worse train service than Bordesley. It is still open, you can buy a train ticket to there, but there just aren't any trains. The people of Barlaston have a permanent rail replacement bus service.

It is a regular bus service that serves Barlaston (along with neighbouring Wedgwood, which is also devoid of trains) and has come from Stoke station and carries on to Stone station to provide rail connections in both directions. It accepts rail tickets too. Although, as far as I can make out, not many.

The bus cannot sell any train tickets, there is no provision to buy or collect them at Barlaston, so anyone turning up must buy a bus ticket. To be fair though, you are unlikely to have just turned up at Barlaston, you would have needed to get there somehow.

Every so often there is an announcement that they hope to start trains again. But they never have so far. The trouble is the bus rather suits the locals. Most of them are elderly and have free bus passes, which they could not use on the train. The bus also goes to the town and city centres, rather than just the rail stations. Stone rail station is on top of a hill and a walk away from the town centre, getting the bus into town is much better.

And so Barlaston rail station limps on; open, but without trains. No one else presented a train ticket on the bus I was on, although it is, of course, impossible to say how many would get the train instead. The bus used to serve Norton Bridge station too, but that did get officially closed.

The surprise with Norton Bridge is not so much they wanted to close the station, but that they ever built one in the first place. To call Norton Bridge a hamlet is to make it sound like there is something there. Unless cows fancied a day out, it is hard to see who else might have ever caught a train there.

Ironically, the reason Norton Bridge closed, was because it no longer had a bridge. The platform forms an island in the middle of the tracks. The bridge from the road to the platform, over the tracks, was removed in 2004 to give improved clearance for larger freight trains. The number of passengers using the station was not great enough to justify building a new one. The station limped on, without trains, for another thirteen years before it was formally closed in 2017.

Meanwhile, on my epic quest, I was on to letter three, and country two. C took me to Cardiff Central in Wales.

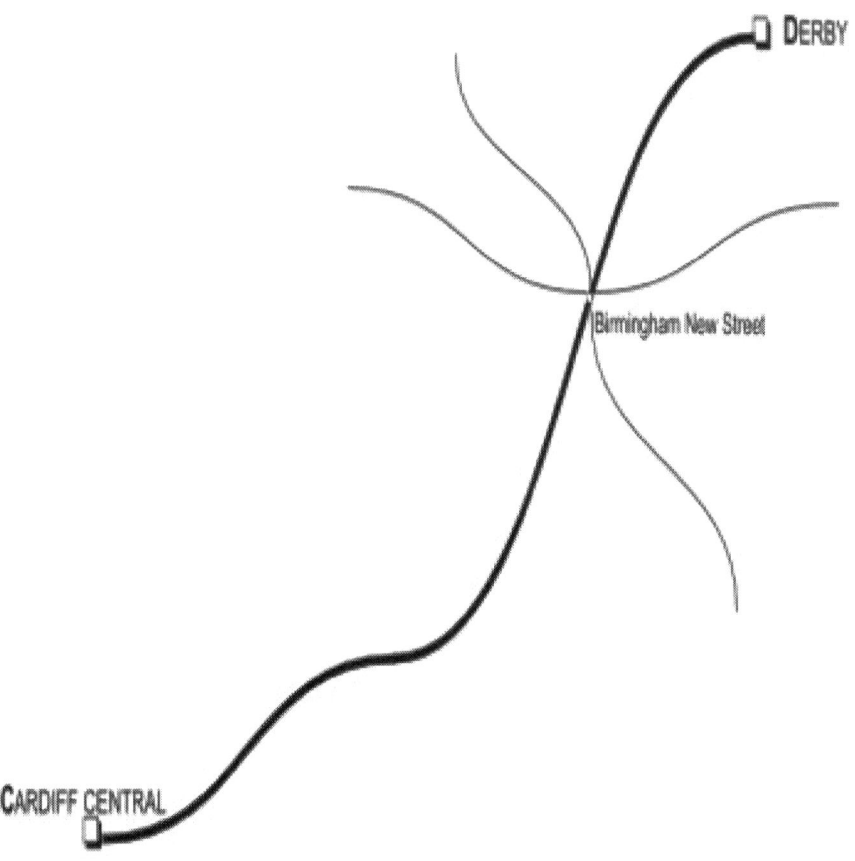

C

A joke I will sometimes tell, if the occasion demands, or there is a lull in conversation at dinner parties, is "I can say the name of the big station in Wales." I pause whilst people assume I mean Llanfairpwllgwyngyllgogerychwyrndrobwllllantysiliogogogoch then deliver the punchline, "Cardiff Central." I am not pretending it is a great joke, but it usually gets at least a titter.

Of course, it is also true. Cardiff Central is the biggest station in Wales. And also, Llanfairpwllgwyngyllgogerychwyrndrobwlllllantysiliogogogoch is not actually called that. It is, officially, called Llanfairpwll. Tourists arriving by train are often disappointed to find that printed on their tickets. But fear not, the tourist shop next-door to the station sells fake tickets with the long name on. It also sells everything else you can imagine with the long name on too.

Most tourists arrive in coaches anyway. They pull up at the shop, disgorge their loads into the shop, and then they pile back on with bursting carrier bags a few minutes later. The sparse train service that calls at the station leaves you stranded there for a few hours. Other than the tourist shop there is little else to do there.

Most trains direct from Birmingham New Street to Cardiff Central go on the direct route. But one a day goes via Bristol; this is the one I was on.

My reason was two-fold. It was the cheapest one when I bought the ticket, and it went through the Severn Tunnel. The tunnel was, until HS1 and the Channel tunnel, the longest underwater tunnel in the world and the longest tunnel in Britain.

It is over four miles long and it takes just under four minutes to travel through. But for safety only one train in each direction is allowed in at any one time. Even so, an average of two-hundred trains a day use it.

Worryingly, the tunnel naturally fills with water. They pump out over fifty million litres of water every day. Should the pumps fail, it is estimated the tunnel would flood in twenty-six minutes. Or six and a half trains.

Whilst in the tunnel you cross from England to Wales. When you emerge into daylight again, all the station signs are bi-lingual. Some station names are remarkably similar in the two languages, others bear no resemblance at all. Cardiff Central is somewhere in-between, with Caerdydd Canolog.

Cardiff Central has eight platforms, numbered 0, 1, 2, 3, 4, 6, 7 and 8. Maybe the Welsh for 5 is 0. The current station buildings date from the 1930's and the original glazed tile wall coverings still show directions to the now defunct platform 5. But not the more modern platform 0.

Cardiff Bay is a waterfront development, and the location of the Welsh Assembly offices. Cardiff Bay has its own railway station now too. The Welsh Assembly pay for a train to run between Cardiff and Holyhead, so their members can travel easily, the only English station it calls at is Chester. They also pay for it to have First Class and a restaurant. But, strangely, not for it to run to Cardiff Bay.

Between Cardiff and Cardiff Airport lies the town of Barry, and its seaside resort of Barry Island. When I was a toddler, we holidayed at the Butlins on Barry Island. It was the last Butlins holiday camp to be built, in 1966, and the smallest. But Billy Butlin said it was his favourite. It closed as a Butlins in 1986, and as a holiday camp in 1996. It is now a housing estate. But there is a blue plaque marking the Butlins camp, paid for by former redcoats.

Nowadays, Barry Island is known as the home of Stacey and Nessa in 'Gavin & Stacey' but it has also found fame in episodes of Dr Who. One thing it does not tend to brag about is the fact it is where the serial killer Fred West ashes are scattered.

Back at Cardiff Central I am waiting for the train to Derby. The station announcements are made in Welsh then English. It makes for long, almost non-stop announcements. Whilst it is important to ensure language and tradition do not die out, as only nineteen percent of people in Wales speak Welsh, it does seem overkill that all station signs are bi-lingual and all announcements are made twice.

The signs and announcements are not even helping, ten years earlier, twenty-one percent of people in Wales said they spoke Welsh. Whatever encouragement people need to speak Welsh, making them listen to train announcements is not helping.

Meanwhile, my train came, and took me to its home.

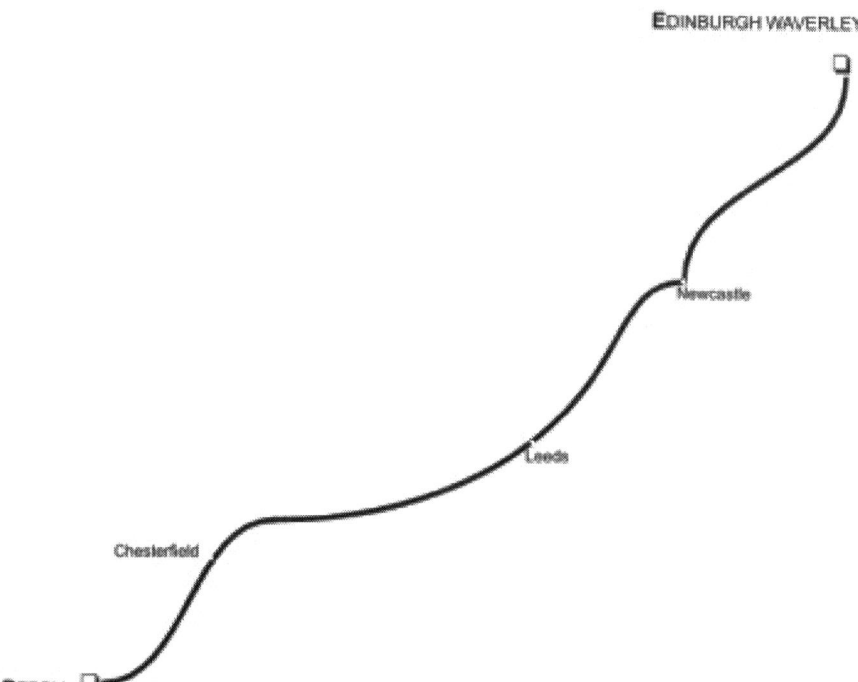

D

Derby has claim to be one of the birthplaces of the industrial revolution. When the railways started, Derby got in on the action. For many years Derby was the only place in Britain building trains, including the one I had just arrived on.

As the train approached Derby station it passed the railway works. Not only do they build trains, they also do a lot of research and maintenance there too. There is also a train depot where the trains retire each night after a hard day's work.

Every station in Britain is owned by Network Rail, but apart from a few major ones, such as Birmingham New Street, the day to day running is undertaken by the main train operator. There are, of course, a handful of exceptions. One of which is the station before Derby. Burton on Trent station is managed by East Midlands Railway, but none of their trains stop there. Only Cross Country Trains stop there. It is just another curiosity of Britain's railway system.

By the time I got to Derby I was getting a bit peckish, so I left the station in search of sustenance. To exit Derby station, you must first go on to the footbridge, you can then exit at either end of the bridge. I followed the signs for the Pride Park exit. That was a mistake.

Pride Park is the home of Derby County football team, it is also home to a lot of offices, including those of East Midlands Railway, who manage Derby station and its signage. I thought about dropping in and letting them know what I thought of their signage, as Pride Park did not appear to be home to any shops or eating establishments.

I made my way back into the station, across the footbridge, and out of the main exit. This was a much busier exit, there were cars and buses and a general feeling you were not in a deserted ghost town.

Derby centre is a fair walk from the station, and I did not have time for that, I contemplated getting one of their yellow cabs, the only feature Derby and New York share, but it seemed over extravagant. I was saddened to learn after my visit that Derby council are changing the colour scheme of their taxis to the more traditional black-albeit with a yellow diagonal stripe-as taxi drivers found the cost of painting their taxis yellow to be too much. So now Derby and New York have nothing in common. Unless they rename Pride Park to Central Park.

There was, however, a chip shop opposite the station, called the Station Fish Bar. It was sandwiched between an off license called 'Mr Booze Express' and a pub called 'The Merry Widows'. The logo for Mr Booze Express had been cunningly designed to look like the Tesco Express logo, but with enough difference to keep the lawyers happy. Although I really could not see anyone thinking Mr Booze had in some way got an affiliation with Tesco. If your name is Mr Booze, you are probably always going to be destined to own an off license.

The problem I had now was the Station Fish Bar did not accept card payments and I did not have much cash. I could go back to the station, which had a cash machine, but time was ticking away.

In the end, I carefully added up what cash I had, and ordered based on price. I handed over my assortment of change and the spotty teenager who was serving had to recall all their customer service training not to recoil in horror at the extra work they were being put to, to add up and sort out this pile of coinage. I am sure Mr Booze would have had my money. They were nice chips though.

Back across the road and back into the station once more. For all the dark and gloom of Birmingham New Street, Derby station is the complete opposite. It is light, bright and airy. No danger of getting diesel fume poisoning here.

I would be travelling with Cross Country Trains again and staying onboard to the train's destination, and my fifth station and third country. I was off to Edinburgh.

Fittingly, the coaches on this train were also built in Derby, although the engines had been built at Crewe. The train is officially a class 43 but is most famously known as the High Speed Train (HST), InterCity 125, as they were the first trains to regularly travel at 125mph in passenger service. The type still holds the diesel train world speed record, set at 148.5 mph in 1987.

The trains have seen a few refurbishments and repaints over the years but are still going strong. These trains are nearly as old as me. I remember them from my childhood. Back then you could open the window and stick your head out at 125mph. A few accidents later, and the windows are now sealed. It took nearly forty years, but eventually common sense prevailed.

I travelled onwards, heading ever northwards. Passing the crooked spire of Chesterfield cathedral. Through Sheffield, York, Durham and Newcastle before arriving in Edinburgh Waverly station.

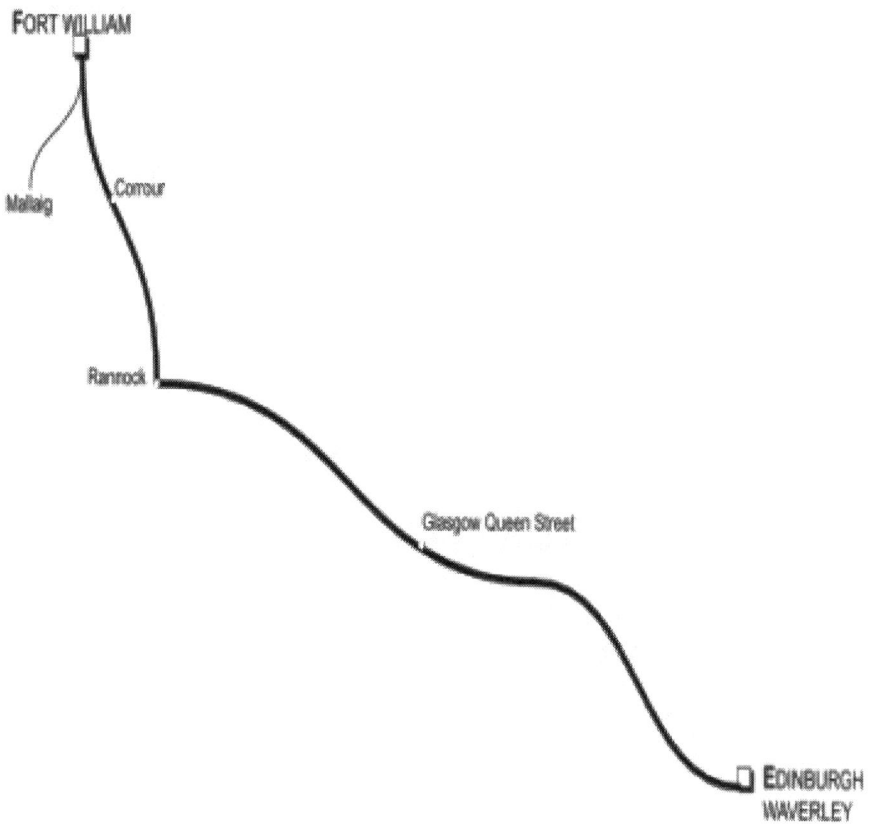

E

Edinburgh Waverly station is in the heart of the city and they have resisted the urge to build a shopping centre on top of it. Although possibly only because there is a covenant on the land which prevents any upward extension, as it would block the view of Arthur's Seat. Although the station has several dead-end platforms, it also has six through ones. Half of the through ones are divided into two platforms. Unlike Birmingham New Street, here they have gone for different numbers, rather than 'A' and 'B' ends. Other than platforms 8 and 9, which have 'W' and 'E' ends. Although it turns out that means 'West' and 'East'.

At first glance, the numbering system seems slightly odd. One end of the platform is 1, the other 20. One end is 2, the other 19. One end is 7, the other 11. But once you realise the numbers run down the East end of the station 1-9, then back up the West end 9-20, it starts to make more sense. Also, the platforms are long enough to accommodate a full train, without the need to take up two platforms. Well, all except one train anyway.

The Caledonian Sleeper train is the longest train to run in the UK. Actually, it is several trains. Each night, two sixteen coach trains leave London Euston, and each morning, two sixteen coach trains arrive. But a complex shunting and splitting manoeuvre takes place in and around Edinburgh in the early hours and ultimately the two Northbound trains serve five destinations. My F was one of them, so I had to wait till the early hours. It was time to explore Edinburgh.

The buses in Edinburgh only accept the correct fare, so tourists like me must resort to begging around fellow passengers to swap money so I ended up with the right amount. I see no real need for there to be no change given, like everywhere else does, but if you really insist on doing it then at least tell your passengers in advance what the fare is to give them a sporting chance of having the right money.

Armed with the right fare, I could stop begging and the bus set off. The city streets were clogged with traffic, Edinburgh, at great expense, had a tram system installed to ease congestion. From where I was sat it was a waste of money.

Edinburgh is a fairly compact city, but also rather hilly. Towering above the city is the castle, perched high on a rocky outcrop, it gave expansive views. You can see why they thought to build a castle there. I had not realised that Edinburgh was so close to the sea, you could see it in the distance, and the famous Forth Bridge.

Arthur's seat is about a mile from Edinburgh Castle and is an extinct volcano, which is an easy climb, close to the city centre and gives great views. It is therefore very popular. It forms part of Holyrood park. Holyrood Palace is the Queens official residence when in Scotland. She can take the Royal train to Edinburgh Waverly and be met on the platform by the Royal car, as there are road ramps down to some platforms. Although, unless you are picking the Queen up, you are not generally allowed to drive down them anymore.

The former Station hotel, now called the Balmoral Hotel-even though Balmoral is one hundred and fifteen miles away-has an unusual claim to fame. When originally built in 1902 it was called The North British Hotel and had its own entrance direct into the station, so its patrons did not have to venture outside. But they did not want them being late for their trains. The solution was to make the hotel clock run three minutes fast. To this day, the hotel clock is still three minutes fast-apart from New Years Eve at Midnight when it is corrected-and the clock in the tower shows the incorrect time to everyone who looks. But at least you do not miss your train.

Back at Waverly station in the early hours and the station is deserted apart from men in Hi-Viz orange jackets. Earlier on, the Southbound sleeper trains arrived. One portion from Aberdeen, one portion from Inverness and one from Fort William. They were combined into one long train to head South.

With eight coaches from Inverness (six sleeping coaches, one Lounge coach and one seated coach), six from Aberdeen (four sleeping coaches and one each Lounge and seated) and four from Fort William (two sleeping and one each Lounge and seated), it is a neat trick to make that into a sixteen coach train.

Why not make an eighteen-coach train? Because the platforms at London Euston are simply not long enough. The solution is to re-move the seated coach and Lounge coach from the Fort William train on arrival in Edinburgh. Through passengers in the seated coach must wake up and move into the Aberdeen portion seated coach. The sleeper passengers wake up to find they must use the Aberdeen portion Lounge carriage for breakfast.

Heading North, the reverse happens. The two coaches are added to the Fort William train and sent back from whence they came.

The sixteen-coach train pulled into platform 7. And a bit of 11. A diesel locomotive was attached to the rear of the train, the rear eight coaches were uncoupled from the rest of the train and it set off for Inverness. Then another diesel locomotive backed onto the new rear, and attached to the next six coaches, and set off for Aberdeen. But not before those in the seats for stations to Fort William had woken up and got off onto Edinburgh station in the middle of the night. There were two of them. We waited whilst a third diesel locomotive backed onto the remaining four coaches, bringing two coaches with it. There was lots of shouting and flashing torches before the coaches banged onto the rear of the train. I guessed most of the sleeper passengers were awake too now.

The three of us got on and found seats. According to the time-table, the website and anyone and everyone you ask, this train from Edinburgh to Fort William has compulsory reservations. If you do not have a reservation for it, you cannot travel on it. A wonderful theory, but an impossible reality.

I had emailed the train company in advance, but they said they were unable to issue a reservation unless I purchased the tickets from them; and I already had a ticket. I asked at my local station at home, but they could not access the reservation for this ser-vice. In the end, I took a punt that the train would not be full, and I could argue a case to be let on without a reservation if there were empty seats. With only three of us, it turned out there was more than enough room and a cover story was not needed. The other two did have reservations, as they were a continuation of the journey from London. It was starting in Edinburgh that was the problem.

Although I was tired, I usually do not fall asleep easily in these situations, and I was right. I stayed awake quite some time watch-ing the dawn slowly break. But as the scenery improved and it was worth staying awake for, I soon nodded off.

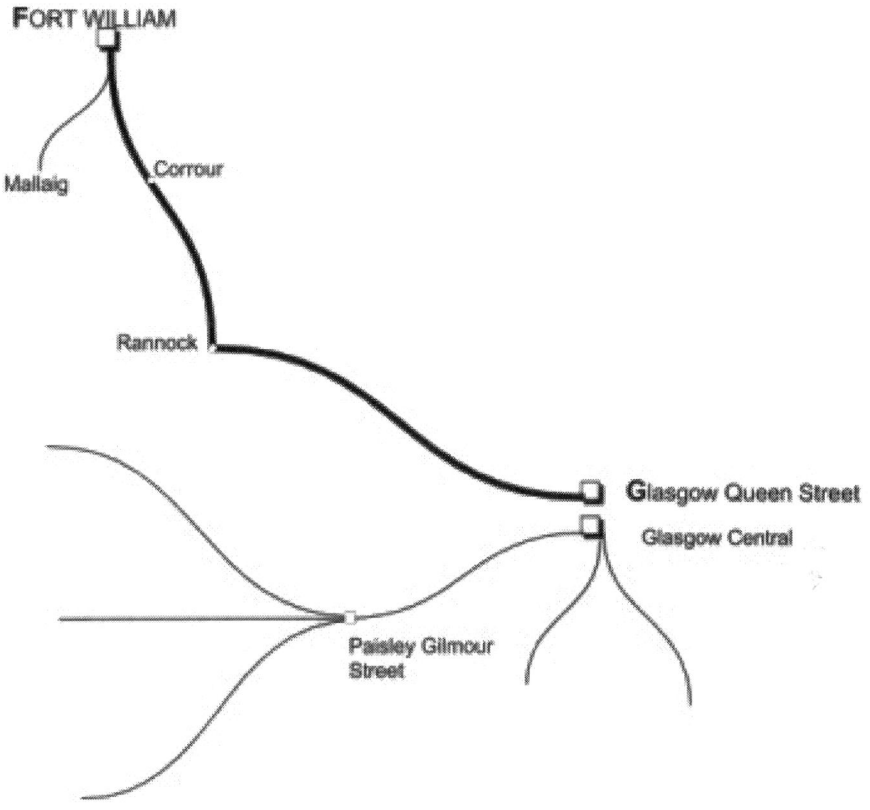

F

The train arrived into Fort William, it has only two platforms, either side of an island. On the other platform was a steam engine and some authentic old-fashioned carriages. This performs two trips a day to Mallaig. Both the route and the train found fame as The Hogwarts Express in the Harry Potter films. It is as popular as it is expensive.

There were really two types of people on the sleeper train. Those that come to go walking, and those that come to ride the steam train. I was the odd one out, no one else was travelling round in alphabetical order.

I had not had much sleep. The other two passengers had alighted somewhere previously, at an improbably remote station. They looked like walkers, most probably off to climb a mountain range, or two, before getting the train back that evening. Other passengers had got on, it is really a local train once it has cleared Glasgow, but I was never in danger of not having a seat.

I stayed to watch those boarding the steam train. Sleeper passengers having enjoyed a night in a bed, and a breakfast in the Lounge enjoying the views passing-by were looking a lot better than I felt. First Class passengers were going to enjoy another breakfast on the way to Mallaig, and a cream tea on the way back.

My breakfast was in Morrisons next to the station. Feeling better for food and coffee I had a little explore. There is not too much to Fort William, it is nice enough and anywhere is improved when you can see mountains from the town, and there is a waterfront.

Most people, of course, come for Ben Nevis. That is reflected in the tourist industry. You can never be unable to get waterproofs in Fort William.

My next journey took me back to Glasgow. The West Highland line has been voted the most scenic in the world. The line climbs out of Fort William up to the highest station in the UK, Corrour. A remote spot, and where they filmed the scene from the film Trainspotting. It is, literally, miles from anywhere. There is not even a road to the station, just a mere track. At the end of that is a road, but even then you are still miles from anywhere.

The line passes over Rannoch Moor, a peat bog that the railway line must float on, using turf and brushwood rather than a solid base. It did not sound particularly safe to me, but the railway has been here since 1894 and not sunk yet.

North of Tyndrum, and budget restraints are nothing new. The railway builders did not have the money for a viaduct across the mouth of a broad valley. The result is the famous 'horseshoe curve', where the line enters, circles and leaves the glen at the foot of Beinn Dorain.

Then it is down to Tyndrum, the smallest and most Northerly place in Britain with two stations, we call at Upper Tyndrum. Tyndrum Lower is on the line to Oban, which we meet at Crianlarich.

Then it is through Helensburgh and into the Glasgow suburbs to Queen Street station, one of Glasgow's two stations. Queen Street has terminus platforms, where we arrive now, and underground through platforms, where I passed through on the sleeper earlier.

I am shattered after the lack of sleep the night before and I have a hotel booked in Glasgow for the night. I have an early night and sleep like a log.

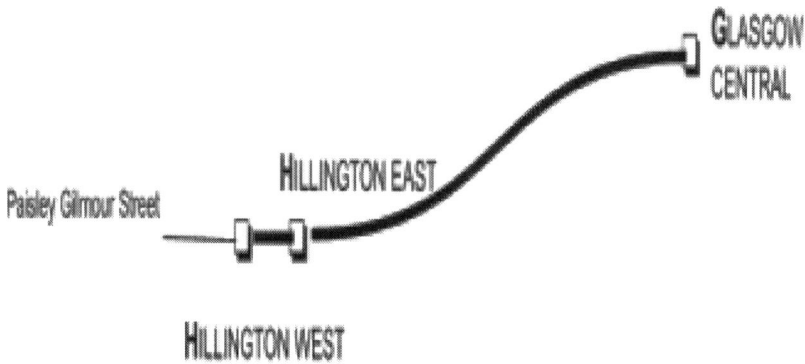

G

Glasgow has an unlikely tourist attraction. The St Mungo Museum of Religious Life and Art. It is free to go in too; I am always interested in a free museum. It claims to be the only museum in the world dedicated solely to the history of religion. But it is probably best not to mention it to the State Museum of the History of Religion in St. Petersburg who might have something to say about it.

It was a strangely fascinating museum. St Mungo is the patron Saint of Glasgow, he brought the Christian faith to Scotland in the sixth Century, which must have been a tough gig. The museum is built on the site of a medieval Bishops castle and, according to them, is built "in its style" although exactly what this meant I do not know.

The museum was simply brilliant and far better than its name might have you to believe. I am not an art sort of person, and I might have skimmed through the galleries, but there is still plenty to see.

It also has a café, which opens out onto Britain's first Zen garden. Most people just sat at the tables though and not cross-legged on the ground.

As if the museum was not enough, across the road was the oldest house in Glasgow with its medicinal herb garden and next to that Glasgow cathedral. It is officially called St Mungo's cathedral. It is both the oldest building in Glasgow and the oldest cathedral in mainland Scotland, suggesting that an island is hiding an older one somewhere. Most excitingly, the tomb of St Mungo himself is in the lower crypt. He is not the only famous person buried at the cathedral. Charles Macintosh, inventor of the mackintosh, is buried there too. If any country needed a mackintosh inventing, it is Scotland.

In the medical garden at the Provand's Lordship were rows of plants all with a list of ailments they claim to cure. I guess in those days-it was built in 1471-you would be willing to give anything a go.

Glasgow Queen Street-where I had arrived-and Glasgow Central are not far apart, so I went for a look at Central station. It is the busiest station in Scotland, with over thirty-eight million people a year using it, of which they estimate eighty percent are passengers. The rest, presumably, are people travelling the country alphabetically and just popping in for a look.

It is a wonderous building. It is Grade A listed and is famous for its glass wall, a feature hitherto unseen. The Central Hotel is an integral part of the station, it has seen several owners since British Rail sold it in the 1980's, all promising to make a go out of it, none of them quite managing to. But it remains a hotel, even if not quite the top-of-the-range one it once was.

Where the station did let itself down was on toilets. When you need to go, you need to go. You do not need to be trying to get the right change because someone thought it would be a good idea to charge. The coffee from the zen garden was no longer having a relaxing, contemplative effect. I asked the attendant if I might use the toilet for free, I showed my rail ticket in the vague hope that as one of the bona fide eighty percent of station users, it might make a difference. He said that he was sorry, but the only people who could use the toilets for free were disabled people. He seemed to be willing me to have a disability, so I said I did. And that was that, I was in for free. Well, I do wear glasses.

Suitably relieved I reviewed my progress. So far, my journey had been relatively straight forward. However, some elusive letters of the alphabet were now coming into play and planning and timing were key.

There are only four stations in Britain starting with J. Half of them in Scotland, one each in England and Wales. Johnstone and Jordanhill are the Scottish ones, Johnston is Welsh and Jewellery Quarter is in Birmingham. Being only one letter different, you do wonder how many people have ended up in Wales when they were meant to be in Scotland and vice versa.

My plan was to travel to Hillington then to Inverkip and back to Johnstone. The only fly in the ointment was that it would require a change of train between Inverkip and Johnstone. It would also need a change of train between Johnstone and my K station. The problem really, is there are just not enough J stations.

Jewellery Quarter would have given me direct access to Kidderminster, so I was tempted; but to get there would require at least two changes of train, so I ruled it out again. Hillington and Inverkip it was. And I thought I could kip in Inverkip too.

Trains to Hillington depart from Glasgow Central, however, in my rules this is fine. Both Glasgow Queen Street and Glasgow Central start with G and I walked between them, requiring no further transport.

All I needed to decide now was if I was travelling to Hillington East or Hillington West.

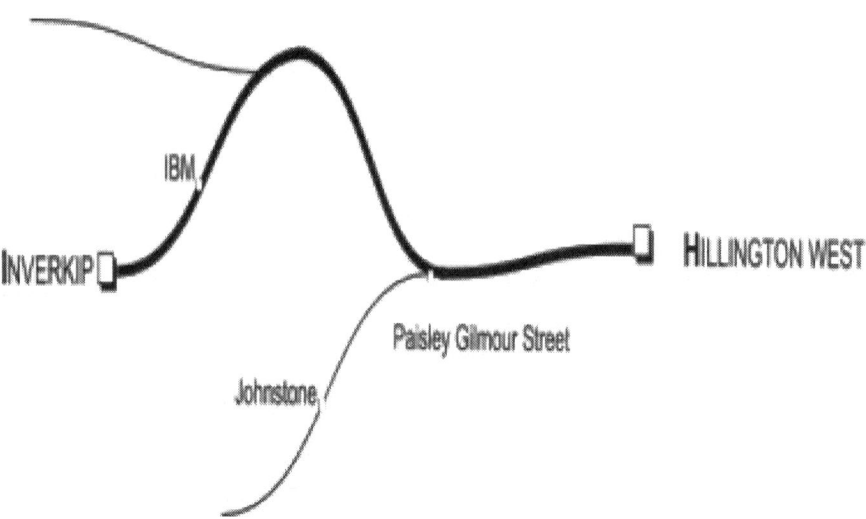

H

Hillington East is the first Hillington you come to out of Glasgow, and I chose to alight here. Hillington West is less than half a mile away.

The railway acts as a natural barrier between the North and South of Hillington. To the North a sprawling industrial estate; to the South a sprawling housing estate. The railway acts as a natural Southern boundary for the industrial estate, the M8 a natural Northern boundary.

I am fairly sure no one has ever alighted a train at Hillington and gone, "Oh! This is pretty." Although industrial estates are usually designed with functionality in mind rather than aesthetics. It was, originally, built as one big factory. Rolls-Royce manufactured Merlin aircraft engines here, it opened in 1937, and Her Majesty The Queen officially opened it in 1938. The first aircraft engines were completed two weeks before World War II started, it is almost as if they had planned it.

They got faster at production, and at its peak the factory turned out one hundred engines in a day. In total, by the end of the war, they had made fourteen percent of the world's merlin engines at this one factory. To keep up with this production they needed workers. The housing estate provided many, the rest travelled in by train.

Hillington East opened in 1938 and was simply called Hillington until 1940. Hillington West opened in 1940 on the same day Hillington became Hillington East and was simply called Hillington until 1952. It must have been a confusing time.

The Rolls-Royce factory slowly retreated, before closing completely in 2005.

Nowadays, the industrial estate is home to various companies and waste land. There is almost one straight road between the two stations. You can exit, and enter, both stations either to the industrial estate or the housing estate. Hillington West even has a ticket office, but it is only staffed in a morning.

I left Hillington East onto the industrial estate and headed West. On the right was a Student Loan office. If there is any money to be made in Student Loans, they do not spend it on luxury office accommodation. Next to it is a bus depot.

After the buses is a builder's merchant, opposite that is a bed showroom. Next to that a balloon factory. There are bland grey units that do not even have a company name on. A petrol station and a bathroom showroom follow.

There is a roundabout now, and a chance to go under the railway and on the housing estate. But I am strangely enjoying myself in this industrial wilderness, so I carry on.

Over the roundabout and there is a competition for tile salerooms, tilemania on the left and crocotiles on the right. I like a pun, so if I were in the market for tiles from Glasgow then Crocotiles would get my custom.

Next, the frankly bizarre "Kilts 4 U" I know it is Scotland, but aren't kilts a thing of tradition and with a family tartan? A company unable to spell "you" never endears them to me.

Mary's Kitchen promised all day breakfasts and special lunch menus. I did not know if the lunches were special or the menus. I thought of going in to ask Mary but decided I probably did not want to know either way.

There were various side roads leading off into the maze of the inner industrial estate, I had ignored them as there seemed no need to get lost to see more industrial units. But the next one was signposted, with one of those brown tourist attraction signs, it read simply, "The Experience".

I did not know if I wanted "The Experience" but I did know I wanted to find out what it was. I set off down the road and away from my route.

I really do not know what I expected "The Experience" to be, but I certainly did not expect it to be an indoor go-kart track. I felt disappointed and let down. It was a bad experience. I turned round and retraced my steps.

Back on the road to the station again and it is not long before I turn into Hillington West station. You cannot miss it; it is just before Caledonian Cremation. I know it says that, I read it three times to check. Their slogan-if that is the right word-is "Simple Dignified Caring" Simple possibly, but I am not sure behind a roller shutter on an industrial estate in Glasgow can be anyone's idea of dignified.

Hillington West station is pretty much identical to Hillington East station. I had not decided if I was going to wait here or walk back on the other side of the track, through the houses, to Hillington East. However, my detour to try "The Experience" meant I had just missed a train, so I decided to walk. I crossed over on the bridge and walked up the path from the station onto the housing estate.

The houses were an unusual design. They looked like they had been designed and at the last minute someone had gone "Oh no, we missed a bit" and an extra bit had been thrown on the front and side. Still, they seemed well cared for and the gardens were well tended. They may not be well designed houses to look at, but the people living in them clearly loved them.

After a while there was a gap in the houses as overhead electricity cables went across the estate. Some houses replaced by pylons; the rest given over to green space. It made a nice open area: if you ignored the pylons and did not look up at the cables.

A little while later and the road turns into a dual carriageway, and there is the bridge that takes you back under the railway to the industrial estate. I carry on through the houses to Hillington East station.

I am off to not one, but two adjacent I stations. Although one is shut.

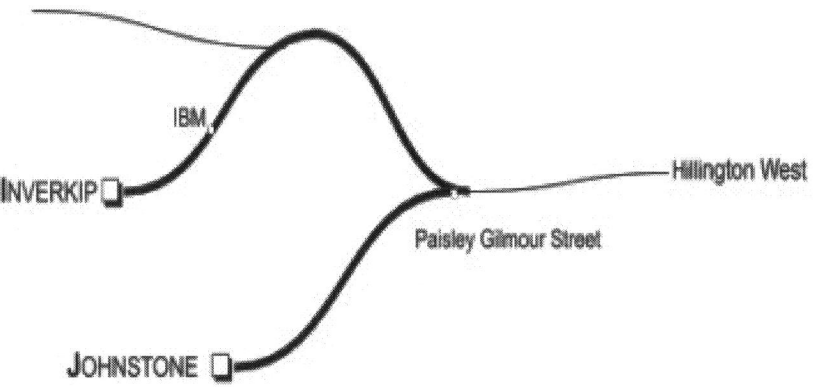

I

Railway enthusiasts get themselves in a pickle over Railway Stations. You see, they do not like them being called Train Stations. You may not mind, you may not feel it matters, but if you do not, you are probably not a rail enthusiast.

Traditionally, it was called a Railway Station because it was where the Railway staff were Stationed. Unstaffed stations were therefore called Halts.

It is not a Train Station because trains are not stationed there. Fire Stations are called that, not because it is where fires start, but because it is where the Firefighters are Stationed. Where Bus Drivers are based is the Bus Station, the buses themselves are based at the depot. Where soldiers stay is called a billet, OK bad example.

Language, however, evolves and develops. These days most people would not bat an eyelid at it being called a Train Station rather than a Railway Station. But call it a Train Station to a rail enthusiast at your peril. The term Halt for an unstaffed station was dropped many years ago by British Rail. Although there does not seem to be a definite date when they stopped using it, we know that by 1974 there were no stations with Halt in the title.

Then, in 1978, they opened a new station. For some inexplicable reason, they included the word Halt in its name. The station was IBM Halt. Guess where I was going for my I? No, you are wrong, I was off to Inverkip. It is the station after IBM, they dropped the 'Halt' in 1983. I would, however, pass through IBM on the way, I would look out for it.

Not surprisingly, IBM station was built to serve the massive IBM offices and computer making factory that surrounded the station. Four thousand people worked there, they all needed to get to and from work; a station seemed the ideal solution.

Initially the timetable was not public, and only IBM employees had access to it. No one else could board or alight there. No one else would want to. The service only called there at IBM shift times. With the decline in the IBM plant came the decline of the station. Some of the IBM site was sold off to other companies, for the first time IBM station was a normal public station. All the trains, apart from, bizarrely, one, now called there.

By 2010 over half the buildings on the site had been demolished, many of the rest were empty. The site was re-branded Valley Park. The station remained IBM.

In its heyday, over one hundred thousand people used IBM station a year. In 2018 it was less than five hundred people. With such low numbers and a rise in anti-social behaviour on the neighbouring derelict land, the service to the station was suspended. The last train to call was the 23.48 to Glasgow on 8th December 2018.

The train sped through IBM station and it is easy to miss if you do not have your wits about you. The next station is Inverkip. It is around two and a half miles from IBM station to Inverkip station, but as Inverkip starts with an I, I saw no reason to walk back there. There are just under four thousand residents of Inverkip and none of them came out to welcome me. Mind you, it had started raining.

Inverkip has a colourful history. From 1640 to 1690 it was involved in witchcraft and witch hunting on a scale compared to the Salem witch trials. Two consecutive ministers of the parish were noted as being 'zealous persecutors of witches.

In 1849 the village crops failed and there was an outbreak of cholera. Over a third of the population died in that year alone.

The village was also involved in smuggling in the late 1700's and early 1800's. Local milkman Thomas Finnie was the ringleader. When he was stopped in his milk cart early on 22nd December 1809 he was found to not only have milk and eggs but also thirty gallons of whisky. On the same morning customs and excise men also arrested another milkman, Robert Cochrane. He had fifty gallons of whisky on his cart. It is a wonder they had room for the milk.

In more recent times, Avril Jones and Edward Cairney of Inverkip were convicted of the murder of Margaret Fleming, for whom they were nominated carers. They lived in a bungalow on the coast. Avril and Edward not only killed Margaret and concealed her death around the time of the new Millennium but went on to carry on claiming benefits for her for another sixteen years. The BBC made a documentary about it.

The bungalow was sold in 2017 and eventually demolished in early 2020. Two months later, planning consent was granted for two new luxury properties to be built.

Inverkip had its own power station, although in fairness it did power other places too. Built in the 1970's it never won any awards for attractiveness, but its claim to fame was reputedly that the chimney was the tallest free-standing structure in Scotland. It is all demolished now though.

I had hoped that the 'kip' of Inverkip was to do with sleeping. The town where everyone has an afternoon kip. But, alas, it turns out it is because the town is on the banks of the river Kip.

The locals have turned this to their advantage though. Kip Marina is not where they go to sleep in their boats, but the first marina to open in Scotland. It even hosts the annual Scotland boat show.

I just need to make a small detour to change trains at Paisley to get to Johnstone. Paisley manages to have no fewer than three stations, but I will only visit the one, and then only to change trains.

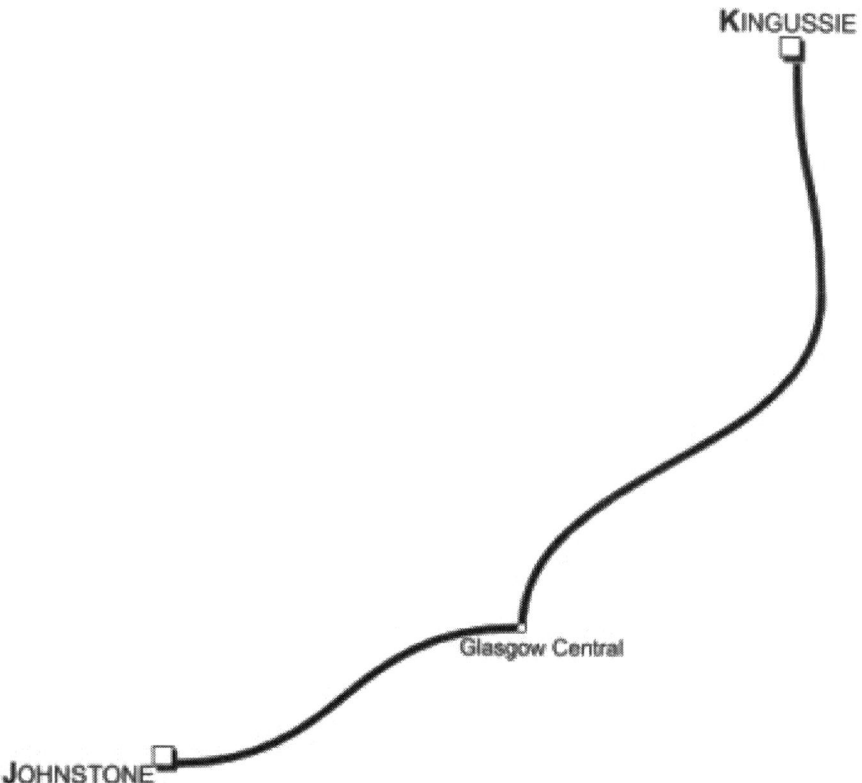

J

And so I set off for the second most scarce letter, there are only four stations starting with J. In rarity value only V has less, with three.

The journey from Inverkip back to Paisley passed once again through IBM station. Plans have been submitted for new residential developments, so it may be that IBM station gets a new lease of life, and probably a new name. Or it might quietly get forgotten about and gently rot away into obscurity.

To get from Inverkip to Johnstone I needed to change trains, and I did so at the station between Johnstone and Hillington West. Paisley Gilmore Street is the busiest of the Paisley stations, indeed, it is the fourth busiest in Scotland, after the two Glasgow stations and Edinburgh Waverly. It has quite a commanding main entrance, designed to look like a castle.

Easter weekend 1979 and a train full of day-trippers returning to Glasgow from a day out at Ayr, collided head-on with a Glasgow to Wemyss Bay train. Paisley Gilmore Street being where the two lines join and hence why I needed to change there now. The Wemyss Bay train was running under green signals, the Glasgow train had stopped at Paisley then left and passed the red signal at the end of the platform.

We cannot be certain why the driver passed the red signal as both drivers and five passengers were killed. (Another sixty-seven passengers and one of the guards were also injured.) But it is widely believed to be, what is known amongst railway staff, as "Ding ding and away." Once a train is ready to leave the platform and all the station duties are complete, the guard presses a bell twice (Ding ding) to tell the driver to go. Although nothing was in the rules to say the platform signal had to be green for the guard to do this, unofficially it was widely accepted that this should be the case. But, crucially it turned out, this was not an actual rule.

Some drivers mitigated against this by putting something on the brake, such as a handkerchief or their hat, if they stopped at the station and the signal was red, to remind them not to go if they got two bells.

Instinct is a powerful thing and it is believed the driver heard the two bells, and instinctively pulled off with fatal consequences. The accident prompted a rule change and now the guard must ensure the signal is green before giving the driver the two bells.

Paisley has four platforms and I needed to cross over to switch from the Wemyss Bay line where Inverkip is, onto the Kilwinning line where Johnstone is.

There are not many reasons to visit Johnstone, but I am prepared to suggest that no one has ever visited before simply because it started with a J.

It is just a town really, not a bad town, but nothing outstanding either. It is not a tourist hotspot, there are not really any attractions. There is a Johnstone History Museum, however its location is more notable than its collection. It is the world's first museum to be located inside a Supermarket.

You can pop out for milk, bread and a brief history of the town. The museum is largely historical documents and maps. Coal mining played a big part of the town's history, and there is a display dedicated to the towns two mining disasters.

There is also a section dedicated to the cotton mill, one of the largest in Scotland. The mill did not have particularly generous owners and the town ended up with slum conditions for its workforce. These continued till the 1930's when housing estates were built.

And that pretty much sums up Johnstone.

To get to Kingussie, my K stop, I needed to change in Glasgow again. So, it seemed a good time to stop the night again there and make a day of Kingussie tomorrow.

It would also mean I could enjoy a hotel breakfast in the morning. A hotel breakfast is a wonderful thing, normally you might have just cereal or just toast. If you are feeling particularly rakish you might have a full cooked breakfast. In a hotel you can have all of that, and more.

I started with the cereal and fruit juice. Then the cooked breakfast. I then made toast. Normally, being asked to cook your own food when you are out for a meal is frowned upon. But at a hotel breakfast making your toast is fun. I put the bread in, and it came out white, I put it back in and it came out black. It is simply not possible to get it brown. But that is the fun.

I then had to spread the little packs of butter that are as solid as a rock. Eventually I give up on the toast and had a croissant instead.

Then I saw a cereal I did not see before so had that and had another go on the toaster with better results. More fruit juice, and a yogurt to round it off. I had to sit a minute before I could stand. Fortunately, I was too full for the prunes.

I waddled off to the station.

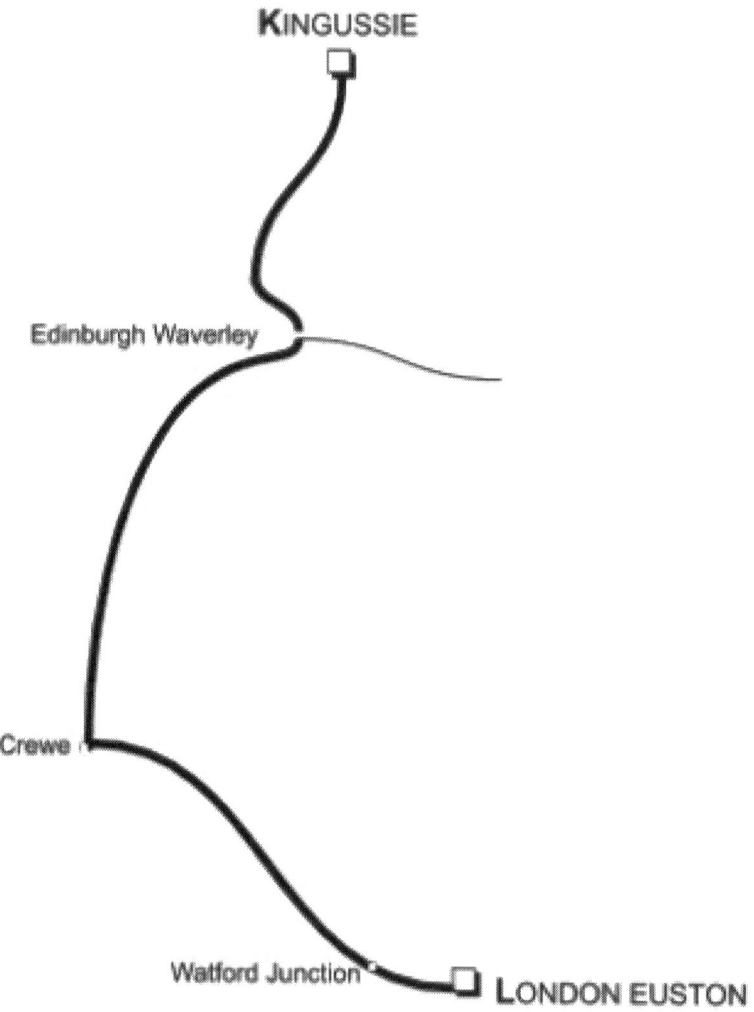

K

The journey from Glasgow to Kingussie gets ever more scenic as it travels on. Indeed, one might say ever more remote too. Starting in Glasgow city centre in the hustle of suburban life it opens out into countryside and then wilderness and mountain ranges.

At Kingussie station both platforms are at normal height. This may not sound noteworthy but has not always been the case. The Southbound platform used to be lower, making it a little perilous for passengers getting on and particularly off. The drop from the train to the platform catching the unknowing unawares.

The reason for it shows the priorities passengers got from the railway builders. It was so the cattle could be loaded into the cattle trucks at a level height and taken off to market. Better for passengers to struggle than the cattle.

Although the cattle stopped travelling long ago no one bothered to raise the platform till 2017. Still, better late than never.

For a city dweller like me, Kingussie seems improbably remote. Snow-capped mountains and a desolate wilderness on all sides out of the town makes it seem isolated, in a good way.

Shinty is a ball game played in the Scottish Highlands that is similar to hockey, in that you hit a ball with a stick, but a whole lot more violent. You can hit a ball in mid-air for example and even tackle another player, but only shoulder to shoulder. These people are not savages. Kingussie shinty team is, according to Guinness World Records, the world's most successful sports team.

Kingussie gives off an air of being a close community and every-one knowing everyone. Word is probably out that there is a stran-ger in town. They probably know what train I came on, where I came from, my shoe size and what I had for breakfast. Although, to be fair, given I had a hotel breakfast you could name any food and be right.

I had a pleasant stroll round the town, there is a free art gallery. But I am not much of an art lover, I feel out of my depth in these places. I am always worried they may ask me what I think of a piece and I will not know what to say. My lack of art appreciation would be exposed, and I would ridiculed for being a heathen.

After the mammoth breakfast I did not bother with lunch; but treated myself to a spot of dinner at the Duke Of Gordon. I chose this hotel simply because it was close to the station. But it did an excellent haggis. I had a little time to kill as I was on the evening train, so made it last. My train was not until just before 10pm. It was only when they turned the lights off and started hoovering round my feet that I thought I had best head back to the station.

For all its remoteness, Kingussie gets two trains a day to London. A day train and a night train. I was getting back on The Caledonian Sleeper, and this time doing it properly with a bed. In fairness I would have had a bed last time if they would have let me; but boarding in Edinburgh for Fort William you can only have a seat. At Kingussie heading to London you can have a bed, so I did.

You really do need to book ahead to get a berth on the sleeper. It is not cheap, you need not only the train ticket, but also to pay extra for the berth. If you do not want to pay extra you can travel in the seats, but I had done that and did not sleep well. Mind you, the other option was a hotel in Kingussie and having seen the prices at The Duke Of Gordon the sleeper did not seem too bad at all.

When the train stopped a Steward opened the door and stepped out. As you must book in advance they are, of course, expecting you. Laura introduced herself and checked my ticket and reservation. I was in the front coach of the eight-coach train. Laura checked my breakfast order, a full Scottish, why not? Coffee? Yes. And finally, what time I wanted it. Probably around Watford Junction would be fine. I could also choose if I wanted it in my room or in the Lounge car, I chose breakfast in bed.

I am never sure on the correct etiquette. Is Laura supposed to wake me in the morning? It seemed a big ask of a young girl. On the other hand, for the cost I would expect a personal wake-up concert by Elton John. I decided to set my alarm for ten minutes before Laura was due to arrive.

It is a strange experience being in a bed on a train. I am not sure if it is being horizontal that makes you feel odd or being sideways on a train. But either way it feels strange. I soon nod off though.

The train goes through the joining up procedure at Edinburgh, along with drop-off calls for passengers at Preston and Crewe and I sleep through the lot. I do wake around five minutes before my alarm though, so switch it off. When Laura knocks on the door, I feign having been asleep to get around the awkwardness of just sitting in bed waiting for her.

I open the window blind to see Watford Junction station. Seeing the early morning commuters bleary-eyed holding onto their coffee cups makes me feel better, still sitting in bed eating my breakfast and travelling at 75 mph. The sleeper does not travel fast, it helps you to sleep better and there is no point in belting along, only to arrive in London in the wee small hours of the morning.

We roll into London Euston, my twelfth station. Halfway. Having gone to sleep at the front of an eight-coach train, I wake at the rear of a sixteen-coach train. It really is a long walk down the full length of London Euston's longest platform.

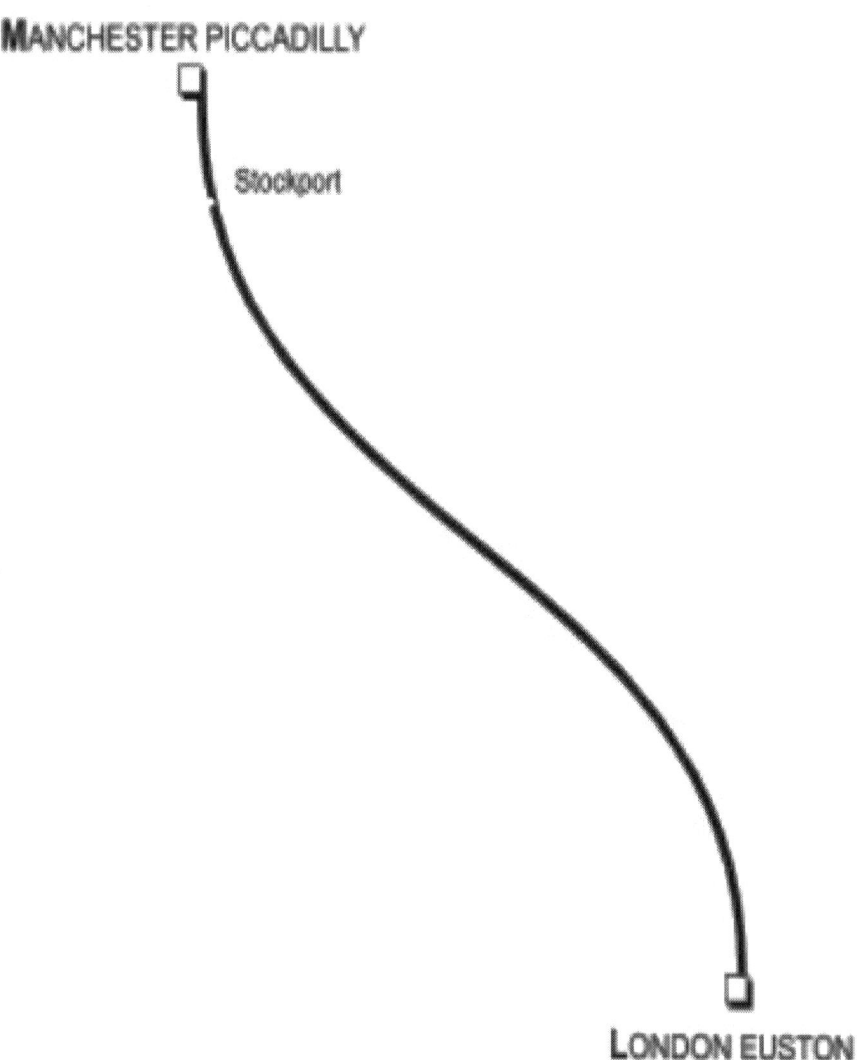

L

London is pretty big. It is certainly larger than Kingussie and you cannot see any mountains from it. I am guessing no one would notice a stranger in town either. After going to bed in the Cairngorms the night before it was quite a culture shock to wake up here.

Sleeper berth passengers can use the First-Class Lounge at Euston on arrival, so I do. Even in there it is busy. I grab a drink, some pretzels and a newspaper and settle down in an armchair.

London Euston was the first London InterCity terminus station to be built. It opened in 1837, named after Euston Hall which owned the countryside it was built in. it was built on the edge of the expanding city, although the city has now devoured it in its expansion. That this was once rural countryside is impossible now to imagine.

The station was built to a grand scale. It had a distinctive stone arch over the station entrances and a Great Hall where the trains departed from. It did not disgrace Euston Hall in its design. A wonder and marvel of the modern age. Not just a practical building but a thing of beauty to cherish.

It was flattened in the 1960's and replaced with an ugly concrete monstrosity that survives to this day. One of the reasons given for the change was that the Great Hall glass roof was dirty and blackened by soot from the steam trains. But as the station rebuild included electrification to do away with steam engines, that seems a bit tenuous.

Just to be sure this did not happen again they made sure Euston did not have a glass roof and instead built a parcel depot on top of the platforms. Thus ensuring the dark Great Hall they were keen to do away with, was replaced with naturally dark platforms instead.

In 2007 ambitious plans were announced to demolish and rebuild the station and add a further three platforms. The following year they added that copies of the original Doric arches at the entrance would be built. In 2011, with the project yet to start, they cancelled it, choosing instead to give the station a lick of paint.

But hope springs eternal, with HS2 planned to use Euston as its terminus, plans are once again afoot to rebuild Euston.

I walked out of the entrance and turned round for a look at it. It is really is ugly whichever way you look at it. On the plus side, it was built to be practical. It has a large area with departure boards where people can mill around and wait for trains. Although if they want to sit, they must do it on the floor as seats are not provided. This does create a trip hazard as everyone is looking up at the departure boards, rather than down at people sitting on the floor.

The platform ramps have large queuing areas where people can wait for the train to be ready without clogging up the platform and getting in the way of cleaners and incoming passengers. However, they choose not to use these now, instead going for the more dangerous 'Euston Scrum'.

Instead of telling you what platform your train is going from nice and early, the departure boards no longer tell you till a few minutes before departure. This means that as soon as the boards refresh with the platform number, they all surge off to the platform, trampling the weaker underfoot. Any notion the British like to queue is quickly dismissed.

But I am getting ahead of myself, I am off to explore London. I wanted to see Leinster Gardens. It is a residential street in Bayswater but has two unusual properties.

Back in the 1860's when they were building the Metropolitan line, rather than boring the tunnel underground, they used a technique called cut and cover. They dig a trench, put the rails in, and then put a roof on it and restore what was on the ground originally. Usually.

As the underground was still steam train operated back then, every so often they needed somewhere for the steam and smoke to vent out of the tunnels. Leinster Gardens is one of those places. To cut and cover they had to remove 23 and 24 Leinster Gardens.

All the steam, smoke and soot coming out was dirty and messy, so they needed a way for it not to pollute straight onto the street. The solution was a façade. This meant the mess had to rise up and disperse. The façade was made to look like the missing houses.

It has been done well, as you walk down Leinster Gardens you would not know they were not real houses. They match the other houses perfectly. It is only when you look for 23 and 24 that you realise, they have no numbers on the door. Then you look a little closer and find they have no letterboxes either.

You look at the windows and find the glass painted a musky grey, you really do not notice at first glance, but suddenly the details fall into place and you realise these are not houses at all.

If you walk round the back to Porchester Terrace, the magic is revealed. A row of house backs, with a gap where you can see underground trains running.

Of course, con men and pranksters have exploited this over the years. In the 1930s grifters sold tickets at 10 guineas each to a charity ball at 24 Leinster Gardens. Everyone turned up in their finery only to discover the house was, quite literally, just a front. Nowadays, local food takeaways are well aware not to take delivery orders for the address unless it is prepaid!

But there is a legitimate business at 23 Leinster Gardens, just in case you do get an invite. As there is no official number 23, the hotel uses it as their official property number, but if someone asks you to buy a ticket for a charity ball there, be aware.

I headed back to Euston in my quest to tick off another letter. I was heading north again now for M.

NEWCASTLE

York

Leeds

MANCHESTER
PICCADILLY

M

You used to be able to get t-shirts that said, "On the Sixth day God created MANchester." They are rather proud of their city up North.

I was travelling on the tilting Pendalino trains. I don't understand the full physics behind it, I failed my Physics O Level, but they say if the train tilts going round corners it can carry on at full speed instead of slowing down for them, thus speeding up journey times.

Again, for reasons I do not understand, you do not notice the tilting inside it. Some people claimed to, saying it was making them feel sick, but tests showed they claimed to suffer from the same effects when the tilting feature was turned off, but they were told it was on.

For this journey I was travelling First Class, so I made the most of it and went back into the First-Class Lounge and had a drink and snacks. Then down to the train and settled in. After we set off, they came down with tea and coffee and to take breakfast orders. It is all included in the ticket price. Naturally, I went for the full English.

Pouring a hot drink is a skilled art on a moving train, and a tilting one at that, but they did it without spilling a drop. Then came some orange juice. The cereal came along whilst they were cooking breakfast. With that finished and the bowls cleared away, out came the breakfasts. Those having salmon got served first, then the eggs and bacon rolls, finally the rest of us with our cooked breakfasts. They placed an empty plate down and served you off a platter of food. Which seemed to make things unnecessarily harder on a moving train.

I asked them if they could give me as much as they could without getting sacked. I was planning to save on having any lunch. My plate duly filled, they moved on down the train. On his way back, he asked me if I wanted him to slip me an extra sausage, which is a line you expect to hear in a Carry On film rather than in First Class.

They came to clear away; and brought down toast and more coffee and fruit juice. By now we were arriving into Crewe, here we turn off the mainline to the North and head to Wilmslow and Stockport.

We waited in Stockport station some time, eventually the Train Manager announced that there was a trespasser on the line so we would be delayed. As the train leaves Stockport, it passes high over the town on a viaduct. Someone had taken it upon themselves to walk off the platform end and down the tracks onto the viaduct. They were now sitting on the viaduct wall. Although not threatening to jump, if a train passed, they may panic and accidentally fall. We would have to wait for them to either finish their walk, or to come back.

As we looked like being some time, they served those of us in First Class with more drinks and a fruit salad. Then more drinks and crisps and nuts and pretzels. After an hour, the trespasser had come down off the wall and the police seized their opportunity and escorted him off the bridge. Finally, we made it into Manchester.

There are four stations in Manchester that start with the word Manchester. Manchester Piccadilly, where I was now, Manchester Oxford Road, Manchester Victoria and Manchester United Football Club. The last of these is not in a timetable and only gets services on match days. I am not a football fan and did not fancy being on a train full of them. But I had heard there were trains running today as a concert was on at the stadium.

What I did not know was if the station took you directly into the stadium and therefore without a ticket for the concert, I would be somewhat stuck. But I would have to cross that bridge if I got to it. It is always hard to cross a bridge before you get to it.

I went over to the platform at Manchester Piccadilly where the trains were going from. Piccadilly has fourteen platforms, twelve of them are dead end platforms, just two go through, these are slightly away from the rest of the station. They had a ticket check in place, but no one asked to see a concert ticket. The train came, there were a few of us on the train, but I would not say it was full.

We arrived at the platform, it is next to the mainline to Liverpool, but on a single line adjacent to it, so trains there do not hold any others up whilst stopped. We all got off. I held back so if I got stopped at least there would be no one else behind.

Fortunately, the station exits onto an area just outside the stadium and there is no need to go in. I slipped off and caught a tram back to Piccadilly. It was a good job I went when I did. Not long after my visit they closed the station as too many people were using it and it was difficult to crowd control. Presumably, everyone still goes so the crowd still needs controlling but someone, somewhere feels better at making this choice.

Back at Piccadilly and I was heading off further North, to the land of the Geordie. I was off to Newcastle.

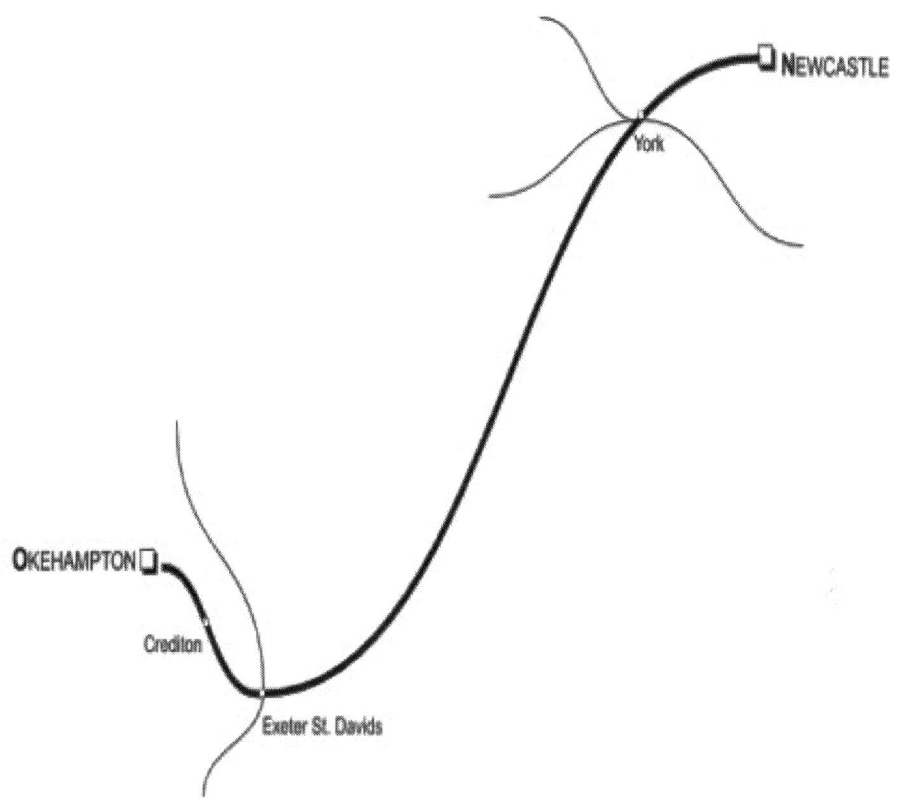

N

As the train to Newcastle leaves Manchester, it is up on a viaduct passing through the city. Down below, you see a statue (for want of a better word) of a bottle of Vimto. Made from wood, there are various fruits and herbs used to make it surrounding it. All made from wood too. It was on that very spot that Vimto was first made. Although now it is part of The University Of Manchester campus.

The statue is called A Monument To Vimto. The drink was originally invented in 1908 by a herbalist who saw it as a tonic, so called it Vim Tonic. It did, of course, get shortened to Vimto and reclassified as a soft drink in 1913.

The train then passes Manchester Liverpool Road Station. This is the world's oldest surviving railway station. So it is a shame no trains call there anymore. It is, however, a Grade 2 listed building and now part of The Museum of Science and Industry. However, it did remain connected to the mainline, so, in theory at least, special trains could still run to the station.

But progress marches on. In 2013 Network Rail announced it wanted to link Manchester's three main stations, and the only way to do it was to sever the one-hundred-and-eighty-year link to Liverpool Road. The museum initially objected, but Network Rail donated an undisclosed sum and the objection was dropped. Now I was on my way to Manchester Victoria.

After the stop at Victoria, we carried on ever Northwards towards Newcastle. At Piccadilly station the Manchester trams run under the station, at Victoria they are on the same level and have their own platforms. They even run alongside the trains for a short distance. They take the shorter route between Piccadilly and Victoria though by running down the road.

The train passes Leeds, York and Durham. In an excellent book called "Heart And Souls" the author talks about an experience at The Queens Hotel in Leeds, it really is well worth a read.

The 'new castle' the city is named after was built in 1080. So it might be time they considered changing the name as the newness has probably worn off now. None of it is left standing now. It was built by William The Conquerors eldest son.

The oldest building still standing in the city is the castle keep, which replaced the original 'new castle' so is actually the 'new, new castle upon the Tyne'. But even that was built in 1175, so it is more the 'very old, new, new castle upon the Tyne' which is a bit of a mouthful to say when Ant and Dec are asked where they come from.

The castle keep, or Newcastle castle if you will, is one of those places where they not only charge you to go in, but charge you extra if you pay tax so they can claim your tax back. I felt £8.80 was expensive enough without making it £9.50 for a 'voluntary' donation. It is funny how the word voluntary has changed its meaning isn't it? It used to mean 'you don't have to it'. Now it means 'you don't have to, but we will make you feel guilty if you don't'. If you come to my birthday party, presents are very much voluntary.

However, from the top battlements you get a view over the station. It is probably why they built it there, so they could see who was arriving by train. Nowadays there is probably someone on permanent look out to see if Ant and Dec are returning home so they can throw a welcome home party.

Newcastle station was opened in 1850 by Queen Victoria. Such was the occasion that Newcastle declared it a public holiday. Presumably meaning that the trains ran a Sunday service.

The station is an impressive building. Simon Jenkins in his book "Britain's 100 best railway stations" puts it in the top 10. And he knows more about this sort of thing than I do. Euston does not even get a mention in the book. Jenkins says of Newcastle "...the station interior is breathtaking [sic]. While Dobson's [the station architect] street frontage is straight, in line with the road, his interior frontage is curved in line with the bend of the tracks. It might be the façade of one of Bath's sublime circuses." Is it just me, or is he coming across as a bit camp there? Needless to say, Jenkins spends two pages enthusing about Newcastle station. To give you some idea, Birmingham New street gets half a page-and not much praise-the best thing he has to say about it is that in 2003 Country Life readers voted it the second biggest eyesore in the country.

Leaving Newcastle aside for a moment, let us turn our attention to our old friend Newhaven Marine.

A station was opened, near enough where Newhaven Marine is now, called Newhaven Wharf, in 1847. Newhaven already had (and still does) two other stations.

The current station opened in 1886 and Newhaven Wharf closed at the same time. At opening, it was called 'Newhaven Harbour (boat Station)' but this catchy title was changed to Newhaven Marine in 1984.

Its aim was to allow ferry passengers to arrive by train and easily board a ferry. It did this well, with the ferry terminal buildings being on the platform too. At the time of my visit, a few years ago, these still stood with a canopy over the platform too. But the platform was fenced off to prevent access.

Unusually for a one platform station, it was numbered platform 3. This is because it took the number from the adjacent Newhaven

Harbour station, which has two platforms.

As the station was, officially at least, still open, a provision had to be made for them. There was, therefore, a poster advertising a phone number to call for ticket holders to get a taxi to Newhaven Harbour station and onward train connections.

There are just two small problems with this. Firstly, you cannot buy a ticket to Newhaven Marine; and secondly, Newhaven Harbour station is only three hundred and twenty meters away. I could see it. I walked it in ninety seconds. It would take considerably longer to wait for a taxi to turn up.

Newhaven Marines downfall started when the ferry service gradually declined and eventually stopped. By 2006 just one train a day was running there. Later that year the station buildings and canopy were deemed unsafe and the platform was fenced off. The lawyers were consulted and realised the station met its legal obligations as long as the train still ran, even if it could neither bring passengers in, nor take them out. And so, the daily empty train started running.

This situation continued for eleven years, until, in 2017, the station buildings and canopy were finally demolished. The empty train limped on for another two years, before engineering works meant it could not operate and even that pretence was stopped in 2019. In early 2020 the government started an official closure process.

In Newcastle, I stopped to take stock and make plans for my future travels. The next problem letter was Q. I had found one that was accessible from a P and onwards to an R. The problem was to get to the P from an O needed me to make a change of train from Newcastle. The obvious choice for an O from Newcastle was Oxford, but this would leave me without a P to Q to. I decided the only thing to do was leave Newcastle and head to Exeter and change there. O here I come.

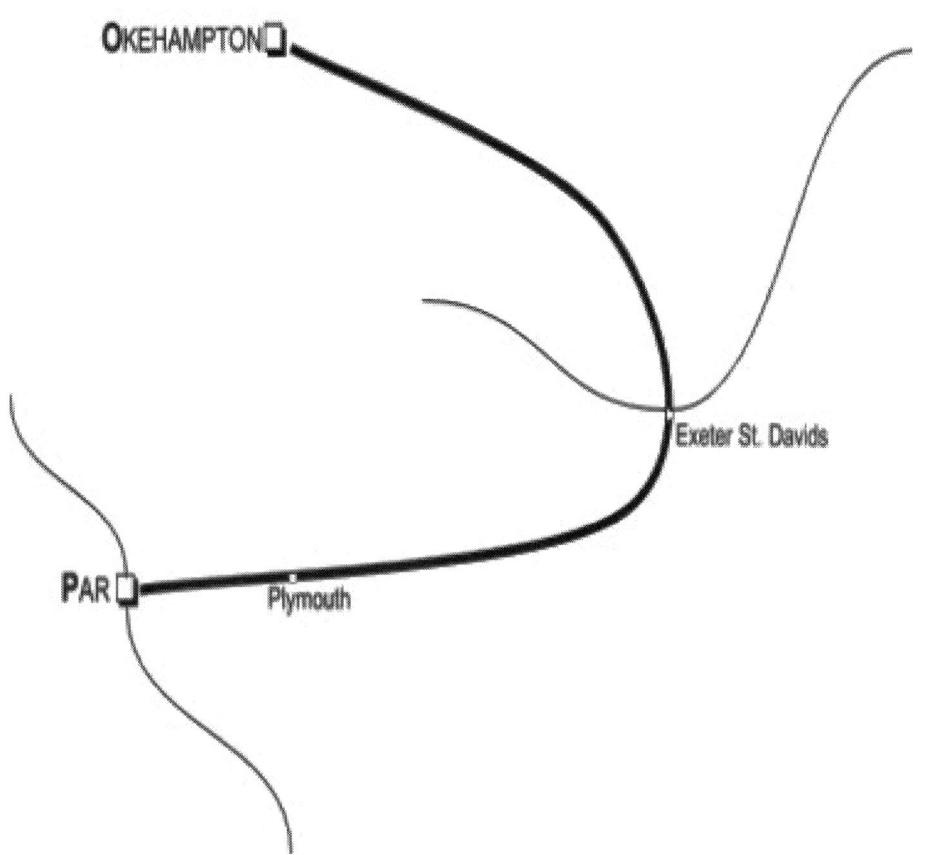

O

I travelled down from Newcastle to Exeter on Friday evening. This gave me Saturday at leisure in Exeter, before venturing to my O on Sunday. It had to be this way, as Okehampton only has trains on a Sunday. And only summer Sundays at that.

Okehampton station is unusual. We have seen stations such as Barlaston still be open and not get trains, but Okehampton is closed and does get trains. It opened in 1871 and closed 101 years later in 1972. Originally the line from Exeter went to Okehampton and carried on to Bere Alston, and ultimately Plymouth. But Dr Beeching cut the line back simply to Okehampton initially, and then completely. Bere Alston to Plymouth still survives as part of the Gunnislake to Plymouth branch.

To be fair, the whole line from Exeter to Okehampton did not shut. Only the bit from Yeoford to Okehampton did. Exeter to Yeoford, and onwards to Barnstable is still open. The line from Crediton onwards is single track to Barnstable. The line to Okehampton from Crediton is also single track. So, although looking like a twin track railway, they are in fact two single track railways side by side. Only at Crediton do they join. At Yeoford they go their separate ways, the Okehampton platform being no longer in use, only Barnstable trains can call there.

The line from Yeoford to Okehampton is privately owned and not part of Network Rail. This does hamper any reopening plans. Although they have reached an agreement to run the Sunday trains, the other six days prove more problematic.

Although passenger trains ceased to run to Okehampton in 1972, the line itself remained open to take stone from Meldon quarry, just past Okehampton. Okehampton station is just outside the town and up a steep hill so when it closed it was just left to sit there. Too far out for vandals to reach to get damaged. The quarry trains stopped in 2011.

In his book "Discovering Britain's Lost Railways" Paul Atterbury-of Antiques Roadshow fame-has a photo of Okehampton station after it shut, in which it is deserted and uncared for, but still largely intact.

In 1997 a Youth Hostel was opened in the old goods shed and an activity centre followed. Sustrans opened cycle route 27 passing the station. The Granite Way path runs alongside the railway to Meldon and then onwards, largely on the former track bed.

The Dartmoor Railway was formed and ran heritage trains from Sampford Courtenay, the first station on the line after Yeoford, to Meldon, the station after Okehampton and the end of the line, on Summer weekends. Okehampton station was refurbished and a model shop moved in and a café opened.

Devon County Council then started funding the Sunday service from Exeter for four return trips a day. Operated by the local train operator GWR. The current Okehampton service was born.

In 2008 the Dartmoor railway changed hands and became part of British American Railway Services. The Model shop and café closed, but the Friends of Dartmoor Railway opened their own café and souvenir shop instead.

In 2017 the government announced it wanted to reopen the line from Exeter to Okehampton. It still is not open.

Due to money problems, British American Railway Services have put all their companies, including Dartmoor Railway, up for sale and are not investing any further money into it. In 2020 it collapsed into administration. All things considered 2020 was not a good year for the railway. The coronavirus pandemic meant no trains ran either. It is almost like the station is closed.

But I was here now, so best to make the most of it. My train to Okehampton was very well loaded. We called at Sampford Courtenay but did not need to, no one got on or off. We arrived at Okehampton and the place was buzzing with activity. The café had a barbeque going on the platform, as well as a Sunday roast dinner inside. It was all wonderful.

The station ticket office had been restored to original condition. I purchased my ticket to Meldon, as the Dartmoor Railway still operate heritage trains there and crossed over to the other platform to catch it. Myself and the other three passengers set off on the three-mile trip.

I had in mind to walk a little way down the former railway line and catch a later train back, but on arrival in Meldon the heavens opened. I had come this far and wanted to see Meldon Viaduct, so I bravely battled on.

The viaduct is an impressive metal structure. It uses wrought iron lattice piers to support the cast iron trusses and is one of only two surviving examples in the UK. It remained in limited use until the 1990s when it was deemed too weak to carry the weight of trains. But it is now open as part of the Granite Way path.

The wind was blowing in this exposed spot, over one hundred and fifty feet in the air. It made the rain fall horizontally. I turned round and headed back, catching the same train back to Okehampton.

The sun still shone in Okehampton and I strolled down into the town. In remarkable combined planning, buses are timed to arrive at the station before each train and depart after each one has arrived. But due to my trip to Meldon there were none now.

I walked down the road, Okehampton is a very pleasant town, but being Sunday was largely shut. On the way down I noticed a path back through a park/garden type area. I followed this back, although the hill was no less steep. The train came back into the station, and again was fairly full.

As the station is officially closed, you cannot buy a ticket to Okehampton. Everyone must buy a rover ticket, there are a few that cover it. Some even include bus travel. But this does mean no one really knows how many people use the train. Guesses put it at around six thousand a year; not bad for a station that is closed, many open stations see less people.

P

I needed a P. The trains from Okehampton only run to Exeter, so I stopped there. Exeter is probably my favourite city. It has a Cathedral, historic buildings, a waterfront and is only a short distance from the coast. But it does not start with P. So, it was back onto a train and off to Par.

The journey from Exeter takes you past Dawlish, where the train famously runs along the sea wall between Dawlish Warren and Teignmouth. Dawlish station even overhangs the beach.

The locals are immensely proud of Isambard Kingdom Brunel. His parents won the first two prizes in the novelty names to give a baby competition. In later life he went on to invent a steam powered ship (The largest ship in the world at the time), a portable hospital he sent to Florence Nightingale in the Crimea War, Paddington station in London (still in use) and the first tunnel under a navigable river (The Thames.)

But it was not all success. His broad-gauge railway was not adopted, and we now use Stephenson's standard gauge. His "Atmospheric Railway" for this stretch of line through Dawlish was a disaster. The idea, in brief, required the use of leather flaps to seal vacuum pipes. The natural oils were drawn out of the leather by the vacuum, making the leather vulnerable to water, rotting it and breaking the fibres when it froze during the winter. It had to be kept supple with tallow, which is attractive to rats. The flaps were eaten, and vacuum operation lasted less than a year.

However, trains ran at approximately sixty-eight miles per

hour. Pumping stations, with distinctive square chimneys, were sited at two-mile intervals to provide the vacuum. Only one of these buildings survives. It is at Starcross and now used as storage for a sailing club.

He also designed and built The Royal Albert Bridge over the Tamar between Devon and Cornwall, that I went over after Plymouth. Before that, you pass the Royal Navy Dockyard at Plymouth. They had a submarine out of the water, they really are quite ugly things, but then it does not really matter as you do not get to see that many.

Slowly over The Royal Albert Bridge, next to it is the A38 Tamar road bridge. It is a toll bridge in one direction only. No one knows if you are paying to leave Cornwall; or paying to enter Plymouth. Although you can walk across for free.

We pass through Saltash station, the first station in the county of Cornwall. Or the first station in the country of Kernow if you think Cornish is a nationality and not just a type of ice cream.

Once, when we were on holiday in Cornwall, we got chatting to another family on holiday who lived in Plymouth. They worked in Saltash so had applied to send their children to school there. In the questionnaire about nationality it asked if the children were either white Cornish or white other. They chose a school in Plymouth in the end.

The train rumbles on through the Cornish countryside. Even when we pass a station there are not many houses. Eventually we arrive at my P. Par.

Par has a local shop, and I am pleased to say it is a Spar. Yes, there is a Par Spar. I went in to see if I could buy rhyming things like a bread ted, or a tap bap, but sadly they had neither. If I had known about the shop in advance, I would have asked at the station if it was far to the Par Spar.

I carried on down to the beach. It was possibly the most deserted beach in the whole of Cornwall. Just me and one other family on the golden sands, it was lovely. It is a shame you can see the china clay factory, but if you look the other way, lovely.

The factory sends out china clay in slurry form on ships, although Par harbour is not that deep, so the bigger ones use neighbouring Fowey. The factory owns a private road in-between the two. They also own the railway line between Par and Fowey after it closed to passengers in 1968.

I made my way back up from the beach and stocked up with food and drink at Par Spar as there is no buffet on my next train.

Par station has three platforms. I arrived on platform 1, I am leaving on platform 3 for the elusive Q. To be honest Q was not too hard. U and V were going to be more challenging. There were very few of either; and no U's near any V's. Alas changes of trains were going to have to be made. I did not want to break my own rule, but as the rule said it could be when no alternative was available, I felt a bit better, but it did feel like cheating. I had not had to do it often, so I consoled myself with that.

I sat at Par waiting for the Newquay train. It was only one carriage when it arrived but was still more than big enough.

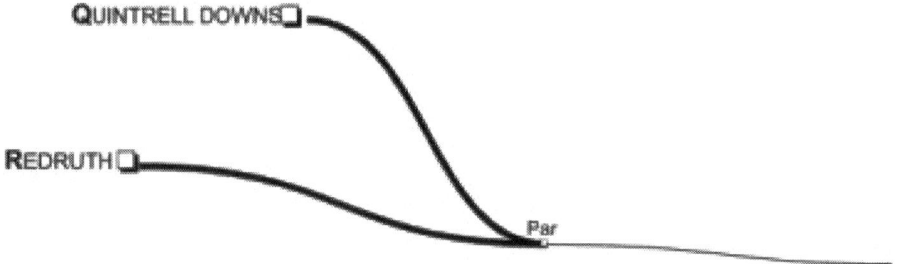

Q

Quintrell Downs is the only station between Par and Newquay that is not a request stop. Heading away from Newquay all trains must stop to activate the level crossing. Even those that do not stop in the timetable, which seems a bit odd.

I was the only person to alight at Quintrell Downs and no one got on. I felt a bit special, only seven stations start with Q and I was the only one at one of them. I do not know why that made me feel special, it just did.

The station opened in 1911 and was called Quintrell Downs Platform. We have discussed the use of Halt in a station name before, and the word Platform in a station name meant a staffed Halt. What is the difference between a Railway Station and a staffed Halt? I do not have the faintest idea.

The staff had to operate the level crossing gates, but in the 1990s it was converted to an open crossing and the staff were dispensed with. In 2004 half barriers were installed and the train crew now operate them, hence the need for all trains to stop.

The station is basic but rather quaint. It is a single platform with a bus shelter on it, but with countryside behind. Downs even. It is rather pleasant.

Quintrell Downs is not a big place by the stretch of anyone's imagination, but it is turned seven by the time I get there, and it is not even the last train of the night. But I call it a day and check-in to the Premier Inn. Places the size of Quintrell Downs do not usually have a premier Inn, but this is, cunningly, Premier Inn Newquay. It just happens to be in Quintrell Downs.

The room was perfectly adequate, but there were no custard creams. I made a coffee from the sachet assortment. There were, of course, those little pots of liquid which bore the name 'Tastes Like Milk'. They do not. I put them all in and the coffee did not even change colour.

The next morning and I partake in the buffet breakfast, then it is off to explore the delights of Quintrell Downs. In fairness, it is nice, but not that big. It is under three miles to Newquay, but whichever way you go you pass open countryside before you get there.

There is a garden centre, but that is about it. But as my train is lunchtime anyway, I don't have too long to kill. There are six trains a day in the week from Newquay and Quintrell Downs. Apart from the summer when Newquay still gets six, but Quintrell Downs drops to just five, as it is a through train to London so misses out all the local stations.

On Saturdays there are seven trains, but in the summer only one of them calls at local stations, the rest are long distance trains for holiday makers from far-flung places like London, Dundee and Manchester.

My train is the only one to travel beyond Par to the West. There is Roche, a local stop on the Newquay to Par line, but there is even less there than Quintrell Downs, so I fancied somewhere bigger. I made my way back to Quintrell Downs station.

I walked the full length of the platform, it did not take long, then back again. I needed to walk off the breakfast, so I did it again.

On the return from my second trip I found another passenger on the station. This was unexpected, for both of us. They eyed me with the suspicion you would if you had just found a man wandering aimlessly up and down a deserted platform. I smiled, which seemed to make the situation worse.

Fortunately, the train turned up before I could embarrass myself further. It had doubled in length since yesterday and was now two carriages. The other passenger waited to see where I boarded, then got in the other carriage.

We travelled back to Par again, there are no sea views to be had on this line. The Landscape is, if anything, more lunar. The clay soil being white, which is why there is a china clay factory in Par.

There was a big disused clay quarry in the middle of the countryside. The BBC used it as the surface of the planet Magrathea when they filmed Hitchhikers Guide To the Galaxy. It is now the Eden Project. It is just two miles from Par.

When the train arrived in Par, it had to change direction to set off for its ultimate destination of Penzance. There are a few minutes wait whilst the driver and guard swap ends and set off again.

There are only two stations in Cornwall that start with R. Roache on the Newquay line, where I had just been to, and Redruth. There are no S stations on the Newquay line, so I decided to go to Redruth.

Between Par and Redruth are two stations. One starts with S, the other T. But there are no Cornish stations starting U, V, W or Y. Alphabetically, I was done with Cornwall after Redruth.

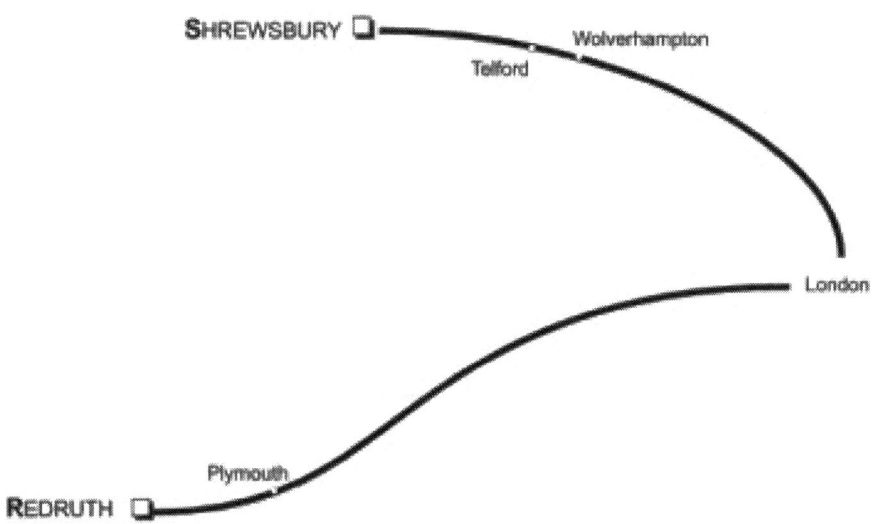

R

Redruth means, in Cornish, red ford. But Red means ford and Ruth means red. That is Cornish for you.

The first station in Redruth was built in 1838, but it was not until 1843 that anyone thought to run a passenger train. By then two hundred people had turned up for it. The train only went as far as Hayle. The station closed again in 1846 when people said it might be nice to go somewhere other than Hayle.

They set about building a viaduct high over the town, and the new railway all the way to Penzance opened in 1852. The original Hayle station became a goods station and the new Hayle station opened on its current site. A railway line linked the two, it has now been converted into a footpath and the goods station closed many years ago.

Isambard Kingdom Brunel designed and built the Redruth viaduct, strangely opting to build it out of timber. In 1888 it was replaced with the current stone one. During the works they operated rail replacement horse-drawn carriages.

Meanwhile, heading in the other direction, the line reached nearly Truro. It could not quite get there till after Isambard had finally abandoned his broad gauge, as the two lines were of different gauges. But, eventually, Kernow was connected to England by train.

Stepping out of Redruth station you come onto Station Road, so it is a good job they built the station there. Opposite you is a rather grey, dreary, uninspiring building. It is the Royal Mail depot. On it is a colourful mural. Whether it is official, or they just have a better class of graffiti here I cannot say.

It has the hashtag 'more ways to talk' at the top and two people conversing in sign language (BSL) with other bubbles round the edge showing BSL signs for hello, yes, no, thank you, please, bye and good. It is a laudable aim, but I wonder how many people have learned any BSL off a wall. But I guess the aim is to promote awareness more than anything. If it is not official it may have been removed by now anyway. You would think Royal Mail would want to promote letter writing.

There was a bus stop and taxi rank outside the station. Both were empty when I was there. I may have been armed with more ways to talk, but I had no one to talk to. I set off down the road and a bus and two taxis were heading up.

The road drops quite sharply and goes under the railway viaduct. But you can veer off too. I ambled round the very pleasant town and came to a Country Health Store, next door to an organic coffee shop. Which promised all things vegan and vegetarian. It used the words vegan and organic in the menu far too often for my liking, so I did not stay.

There are no U's and V's next to each other as we had established, so changes of trains are going to be necessary, so I may as well do it in style. I made my way back to Redruth to get The Night Riviera sleeper train.

The first sleeper to the South West ran in 1877, but only between London and Plymouth. It was also in Brunel's broad gauge. It had two dormitories the gentlemen's one with seven beds, and the Ladies one with just four.

By 1881 this had been replaced with new carriages containing six individual rooms. By 1920 an additional sleeper train was running from London to Penzance. To cut costs, British Rail combined the two into one train, detaching two coaches at Plymouth for passengers to wake up at a more leisurely time. To cut costs further, this practice was abolished in 2006 and if you want Plymouth now, you must be up by 5am.

On the 5th July 1978, the sleeper set off from Penzance as normal, but never made it to London. The sleeper carriages usually attached at Plymouth were in the platform and waiting for the main train. Plymouth did not handle linen, so clean sheets were dropped off each night, and the dirty ones sent back to London each morning, these had been stacked up in a vestibule as was normal practice.

The sleeper train had recently been upgraded, and now included electric heating. The linen had been stacked in front of the electric heater. When the main train joined on to the coaches and the heating came on, it was just a matter of time. The ventilation system sucked in air from the vestibules and put it in the sleeping compartments.

The fire started in the linen and the ventilation system put the smoke and carbon monoxide into the sleeper rooms. Twelve people died in their sleep without ever knowing there was a fire.

In 1983 brand new sleeper coaches were introduced, these did not have electric heaters and also had fire alarms. Lessons had been learned.

These coaches were totally refurbished in 2018 and new flame-retardant materials used throughout. The seated coaches have also been completely overhauled and now have the most uncomfortable seats available on the market. But, contrary to popular opinion, that is not the reason they were chosen. They are the safest seats on the market. They do not snap into sharp pieces if there is an accident, there are no sharp edges to cut yourself on if you lose your balance or get thrown around in a derailment. There are no hard surfaces to bang yourself on-apart from the seat cushion. These seats maybe safe, but they really are hard and uncomfortable.

I had treated myself to a bed though. Jean, my steward, showed me around the small but perfectly formed room. She gave me instructions on how the various light switch combinations worked and showed me the call button I could use to summon her in the night if I wanted. I placed my breakfast order. The train arrives into London around 5am but you can stay on till 7am though. I asked for a 6am breakfast which seemed more than early enough to me, but Jean wanted to be sure I would be up and off the train by 7. I assured her I would.

I went to the Lounge, for no reason other than you get free drinks and snacks and I wanted to get my money's worth. Neil was serving, he was a happy easy-going fellow. I had a hot chocolate and a bag of nuts. I asked what he gets up to once everyone has gone to bed.

"Everyone is never in bed." He chuckles, "or at least not in their own." He winks a knowing wink. "You see it all in this job. You see it all." He smiles at the memories.

I make a mental note to lock my door.

I set my alarm for 5.45 so I can be awake to pretend to be asleep for Jean with the breakfast tray. I did not need to bother as she comes at 5.40 anyway and wakes me. She reminds me I must be off to the train by 7. It is only a bacon roll and a coffee; how long does she think it will take me?

Before I get off, I go to the Lounge car for an Orange Juice from Neil. Being careful to leave my bag on the bed so Jean knows I am still here.

"Sleep well?" He asks.

"Yes, thank you." I reply, "no nocturnal disturbances last night?"

"No, you were a good lot last night."

It is nice to have his seal of approval. It must be an odd life working the sleeper. He is Cornish and lives near Zennor, so today he will sleep in a London hotel and return home on tonight's sleeper, whilst a London based crew do the same in reverse.

I stay in my room till 6.59, just because I can. As I leave, Jean is hovering outside.

"You're the last one." She says. I was not sure if she was telling me off or making a statement of fact.

"Someone has to be." I reply.

"I suppose they do." She says. With that she locked up and went off to the hotel.

Meanwhile, I had to get myself a train to Shrewsbury. There is only one a day, but there was still plenty of time to wait. Sleeper berth passengers can use the First-Class Lounge on arrival, so I did. There are free papers to read to. I felt like a businessman, although I could not decide what business to be in.

Part of the First-Class Lounge used to be Queen Victoria's personal waiting room. It was nice to be in the same league as the Queen. I had a croissant to celebrate.

Then it was off for the Shrewsbury train. I had a date.

SHREWSBURY ☐ TELFORD CENTRAL

S

Eighteen letters down and six to go. I was starting to flag slightly, so my partner Cath joined me with Shrewsbury. It was nice to have company, and hers in particular.

Shrewsbury station opened in 1848, the platforms are nothing special, but the station building is rather splendid and was made grade ll listed in 1969. This building opens out onto the lowest numbered platform. Platform 3. On the wall of the building on platform 3 is a war memorial listing the forty-two railway employees who lost their lives in The Great War. Platform 3 is rarely used, and the plaque is therefore seldom seen by the public.

If you stand on platform 7, you can see the rooftop of Shrewsbury prison peeking over the wall in front of you. Look at the wall more closely and you can see it does not appear to have a function. But you would be wrong, behind it is a railway line and what looks like a platform. This is the platform that trains of prisoners would arrive at to be taken to Shrewsbury gaol. The wall screens the convicts from public view.

The current prison building was constructed in 1877. Ten people were executed within its grounds, the last being in 1961. As was customary at the time, they were all buried in unmarked graves within the prison walls. In 1972 the Ministry of Justice exhumed all the bodies and they were cremated and scattered at the crematorium. Apart from one, which was returned to the family. One assumes they asked for it to be.

In 2008 a report suggested the prison was overcrowded. It had space for one hundred and seventy-eight prisoners and held three hundred and twenty-six. Government money well spent on getting that report commissioned. The cost to sort this out was deemed too great and the prison closed in 2013.

As the building was used to ne'er-do-wells living in squalor and anti-social behaviour it was originally planned to turn it into student accommodation. But the council rejected the plans. Presumably not wanting to lower the tone of the neighbourhood.

The River Severn nearly circles Shrewsbury into an island, but where the station is, there is a join onto the mainland. The town is proud of its local boy Charles Darwin and afforded him the highest honour any town can, by naming its shopping centre after him.

We walked uphill from the station into the town centre. There are lots of maps and signposts, I noted the maps even tell you where there are steep hills to negotiate. Cath and I set off for a riverside location and Shrewsbury Abbey. We had a nosey around the Abbey, the clock on the outside is unusual in that the numbers are set out as if Roman Numerals, but they use "f" in place of the usual "X" for ten.

We had a little stroll down by the river, walking round to The Quarry, which is a large grassy park area and not an industrial mining area. We cut through it and out of the gates into the town, where we spied St Chads Church. We went in for a look, and found the steward, an elderly gentleman, gently snoozing in his chair at the entrance.

We were not sure what etiquette was in such circumstances, but we decided to leave him sleeping and tiptoed past him into the church. Although an Anglican church it was a circular building and therefore an unusual layout. We were admiring the building when the steward woke up and came in.

He apologised for not seeing us come in and Cath said,

"It is OK, you were just having a quiet moment, so we left you to it."

He then went on tell us about the church, its history and everything else about it. I literally took a pew as we were clearly going to be here some time and he felt he owed us this full history to make up for missing us coming in. One fact that did perk me up was that in the graveyard was a tombstone for Ebenezer Scrooge. It is not, of course, a real one, but merely a leftover prop from when the 1984 film was shot in Shrewsbury.

Our guide and new friend was all for coming out to the graveyard to show us, but we assured him we could find it and left him to welcome some other tourists who had just turned up and he was awake for.

After successfully finding a fake gravestone, we headed back through town and down to the river where we boarded a boat for a cruise back where we walked past The Quarry.

The captain was a jolly Scottish fellow with a thick accent. He gave an entertaining and informative commentary, of which I understood not a single word. There were onboard refreshments, often these things are ridiculously expensive, but we bought a small carton of Ribena and a can of Coke and still got change from £20.

Once we were back on dry land, we walked back through the town to the station. We had had a lovely day. Shrewsbury did not suffer greatly from air raids in the war so still has many historic buildings. One of them is now the Public Library, formally Shrewsbury School where Charles Darwin was educated. It was shut for the day when we passed, but we had a look in the grounds of this most magnificent building. It is right by the station, so we went up to the platform to await our onward trains.

Just five letters left and the most complicated bit of the trip so far. I had only had to change trains between letters in three places so far. Once in Paisley, between I and J, again in Exeter for O (both inbound and outbound), and London to get here. I was going to have to change between T and U, U and V and V and W. I guess, all things considered, not too bad. But I still found it annoying.

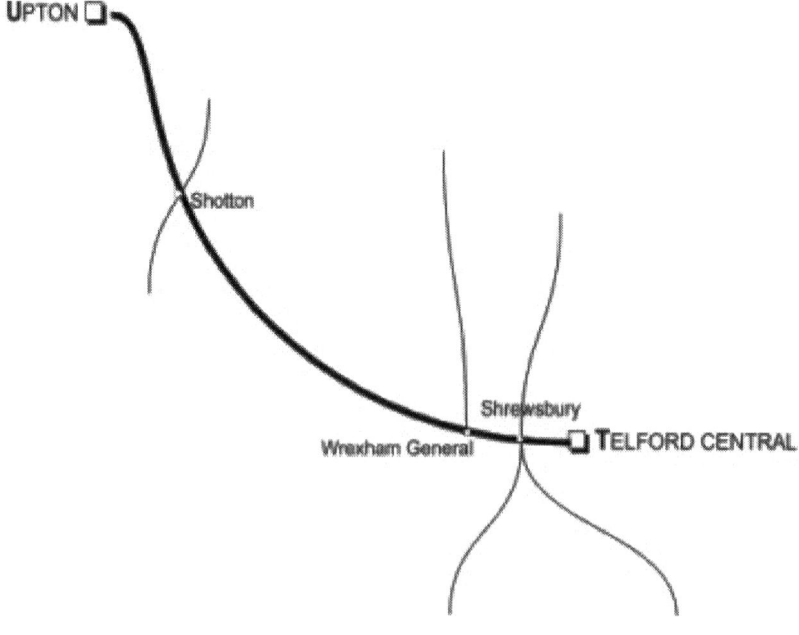

T

Telford is one of the new towns of the 1960s and 1970s. Originally it was planned to be called Dawley, which would have been no use to me on this quest. Other rejected names include the bizarre Dawelloak, and the more helpful to my journey, Wrekin Forest City. Although that sounds like what the local hoodlums might do on a night out.

Telford was first designated, as Dawley, in 1963. With the first homes built in 1967. In 1968 it was expanded and renamed Telford. It does not, therefore, have much history. My siblings have been in existence longer than that.

Eventually, in 1983, Telford joined the motorway network when the M54 connected it to the M6. Just three years later, Telford Central railway station opened. Previously, the existing station at Wellington had simply been renamed 'Wellington-Telford West' to indicate the fact it was vaguely close to Telford.

Telford station can best be described as practical. Sitting at Par or Redruth you can imagine steam trains running through and the hustle and bustle of a bygone age. You do not get that with Telford. British Rail built the station, and they had in mind Inter-City trains calling to whisk people off to London. Presumably thinking there was nothing much in Telford to keep people there.

The trains to London did not last long, and British Rail ceased them in the early 1990s as unprofitable. Why that made Telford different to anywhere else with British Rail is not explained.

Undaunted, when Virgin Trains took over the rail franchise at the start of rail privatisation in Britain, they too started a direct rail service from Telford to London. It lasted less than a year before they abandoned it as unprofitable. Critics argued that this left Shropshire as the only county without a direct rail service to London. As long as you forgot about Rutland; which most people do.

Undaunted, a private rail company was formed to start a direct rail service from Telford to London in 2008. Wrexham and Shropshire Railway tried to resolve the problem of low passenger numbers by including not just Shrewsbury but also Wrexham in the service. This service limped on till 2011 when the company ceased trading due to the service being unprofitable.

Undaunted, in 2014, Virgin Trains restarted services from Telford (and Shrewsbury) to London. This time keeping costs lower by only running a small train and joining to another train at Wolverhampton. Virgin Trains then lost the West Coast rail franchise, and Avanti won it. Part of the new franchise commitment is to continue running the trains to Telford. The future has never looked so bright.

The station may be called Telford Central, but it is not really. You come out and find yourself on the edge of town with a dual carriageway to cross. There is a bridge and it is a nice bridge too. Covered from the worst of elements and with glass sides to make it feel welcome and open. But the fact it is there at all just adds to the feeling of remoteness.

Telford is a nice enough town. It does not market itself as a tourist town. People do not tend to visit any of the new towns created round the same time. When did you last hear someone say, "I am off for a day trip to Welwyn Garden City today"? But it does its function well. I had a wander round the shopping centre and as far as the ice rink. Then off to the town park.

Telford Town park has won many awards and it is genuinely nice to have such a wonderful space in a town. Everything you would expect of a park and more besides. And all in the town centre.

In 1980 The Reverend Awdry, author of the Thomas The Tank Engine books, officially opened the miniature steam Tramway, which ran around the lake. It lasted five years before being moved out of the park, but still in Telford.

A stone throw from Telford (if you are incredibly good at throwing stones) is Ironbridge. Here the first major iron bridge in the world was built to cross the River Severn. Suddenly the potential to use cast iron in construction was realised and thus started the industrial revolution.

The bridge was built here as the area was rich in coal, iron ore, clay and limestone that all needed mining and crossing the Severn. The dirt and pollution from all this can only be imagined. But nowadays it is as if this industry never existed and nature has taken back over and it is a lovely country village, deep in rural countryside.

The nearby Blists Hill open air museum is a village of lovingly reconstructed houses, shops and other businesses, some moved brick by brick here from their original location to create the village of Blists Hill. Although it now appears to be in the middle of countryside, many of the buildings are, in fact, original to the location. Showing that, given time, nature can reclaim even the most ravished landscapes.

With only four letters left to go, my trip was nearing its end. I headed back to Telford Central to await the onward train to Wrexham, which I would come back to as my W, and onward connection to my U. The train to Wrexham was four carriages. The passenger information system was clearly broken. The electronic displays bearing the incomplete message "This train is for" whilst the automated announcements repeated "Welcome aboard this service." But mentioned nothing further. Ironically, as if to taunt me, this train went on to call at my V too. Half my remaining letters on one train, but I had to detour first to U.

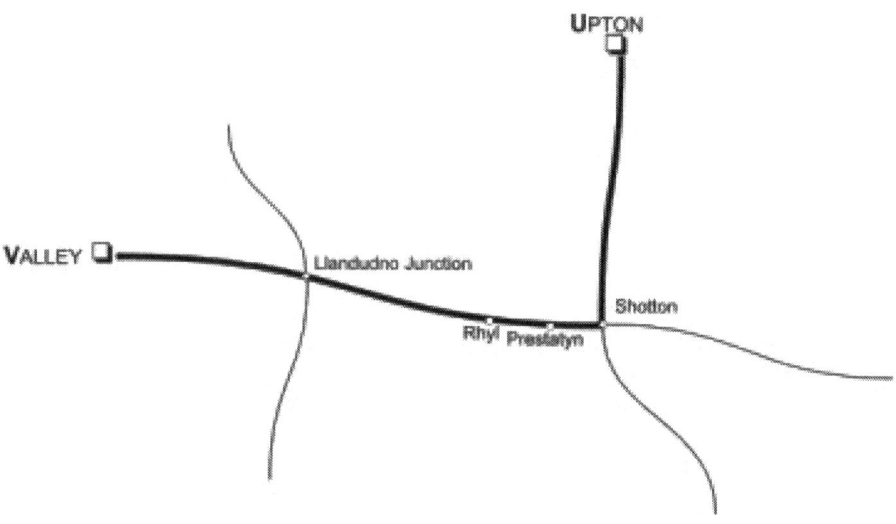

U

A change of train at Wrexham sees me on a two-coach train to Bidston. An unusual place for a train to terminate, but it is where it connects to the Merseyrail network and, as such, stations on my trains' route miss out on direct trains to Liverpool. One of those stations starts with U.

We arrive at Upton. It is located on the Wirral peninsular, across the Mersey from Liverpool. Upton was recorded in the Doomsday book in 1086, so the place is a little older than Telford. However, it still does not look it. There are not many historical buildings to marvel at.

The place grew around Upton Hall, which changed families several times, before being sold to the Society of the Faithful Companions of Jesus (FCJ) in 1862, who turned it into a girls convent school. Back then, education was really just for boys and the aim was to get girls onto an equal standing, at least in education anyway. It is now Upton Hall School FCJ and they still aim to send girls out into the world following the school motto "Age Quod Agis". Which as Latin scholars, you do not need me to translate for you. (Whatever you do, do well)

I was not expecting to spend long in Upton, and I didn't. Although that is not the fault of Upton. I went back to the station situated on a busy dual carriageway by the M53, the platforms however, situated below road level, were peaceful and very green. Apart from the noise of traffic, you could be in the countryside.

I got a train heading back to Wrexham but bailed out before then at Shotton. Here, the line I was on, passes, at right angles, over the line from Chester to Holyhead. I get off and go down to the platform below.

The trains from Telford to my next station are every two hours, I needed to be slick in Upton. The railways first arrived in Shotton in 1848, but no one thought to provide a station till 1891. Dr Beeching decided to close the lower station in 1966, so Shotton residents could no longer get to Chester or North Wales. However, due to fierce local opposition, it reopened in 1972. I am glad it did, as this journey would not be possible had it not.

The train came into view and stopped at the station. Quite a few passengers got off and there were half a dozen of us waiting to get on. The train started its endless bilingual messages; despite us not making it over the border into Wales just yet.

By the next station (Flint) though, we are into Wales and the station names become bilingual too. Flint is Fflint. We carry on and the train starts getting its first glimpse of sea. First as the estuary of the Dee, with Parkgate and West Kirby on the other side, then the actual sea itself.

British Rail used to operate ferry services too and had their own boats to operate them. One of them was TSS Duke of Lancaster. It started off on the ferry route from Heysham to Belfast; but ended up cruising the world, well Scandinavia anyway. However, car ferries were the way forward, so whilst the ferries were being converted, the Duke of Lancaster was pressed back into ferry service again. Initially back to Belfast, but also other Irish routes, before finally being retired in 1978.

In 1979 it was put into dry dock near Mostyn and transformed into the "Fun Ship." The project was doomed pretty much from the start. Although initially located on the main road into North Wales, a new bypass was built meaning there was no longer any passing traffic bringing in potential customers.

Local opposition and a less than sympathetic council, saw the project run into lengthy legal battles. At each twist and turn in the process the Fun Ship had to close. For such a big thing it quickly got forgotten about. Few people got to see inside it, and it sat rusting away into obscurity.

As part of its conversion into the Fun Ship a whole deck was given over to an arcade. Other decks are still in original condition from its sea-faring days. Despite its aging rusty exterior, the interior is still in surprisingly good condition. Although it never had been open much, in 2004 it closed for good.

A chance find of some interior photos online by an arcade enthusiast and they wanted to know if the machines were still there. A lot of phone calls later, the owner was found and, eventually, a deal was struck. Thirty-year-old arcade machines were removed.

In 2012 a new plan was formed to turn it into an art gallery. The outside was daubed, officially, in graffiti art by artists such as Kiwie, Spacehop and Snub23. This plan too, failed. The ship was painted black in 2017. You can still see the ship from the train, sitting there in all its rusty splendour.

My journey continued ever onwards, through Prestatyn, Rhyl and Colwyn Bay. After Llandudno junction the train goes into a tunnel on a bridge over the River Conway. The tunnel part of the bridge was constructed on land, then floated down the river on a pontoon, before being lifted into place.

After emerging from the tunnel, the train passes through the town walls and runs alongside Conway Castle. Although it does not really pass through the walls at all. They had to take a bit down (they had only been there since 1283 after all) and put up an archway for the train in a similar style.

The train continued on, ever Westwards, and just before Holyhead, we arrived at Valley.

V

Valley is a request stop, so I had made sure to tell the guard I wanted to get off. It was the first request stop of my journey, so I had a frisson of excitement getting off that the train was stopping only because I wanted to get off. It was short lived when I realised three other people were getting off too.

Valley station originally opened in 1849. In 1870 they extended the station buildings; they lengthened the platforms in 1889. Then they shut the station in 1966, which seemed a shame after all the work they had done. They set about demolishing the station buildings and platform but had only done one side by the time the station reopened in 1982. Which is why the platform I got off on was new and only had a bus shelter.

I had never intended to stay in Valley long, I was here purely to tick off the V. A quick wander down the road, and back at the station to get the same train heading back. The building may be more substantial on this platform, but it provides no greater shelter as none of them are open any more. However, still being the original platform, it had a Harrington Hump.

There is no standard platform height in Britain. Platforms were built fairly randomly, in the early days particularly. As a result, the Eastbound platform at Valley is particularly low. This makes it difficult for many people to get on and off trains and impossible for those in wheelchairs. The cost to raise all the platforms at all the stations would be considerable, so they invented an "Easy Access Area" or EAA for short.

This involved raising just a small section of the platform with a pre-formed modular system with ramps at either end. Installed in a couple of days and whilst trains were still running, it cost around a tenth of the price of raising the full platform.

The first one was installed at Harrington in 2008, this location was chosen as it was a particularly large drop between the train and platform; it is a coastal location so would be tested in harsh conditions; and Cumbria Council were willing to help fund it.

It quickly earned the nickname 'Harrington Hump.' So much so that Network Rail have now given up officially calling it an EAA. After a three-year trial other Harrington Humps were installed at more stations. They are placed where the wheelchair accessible door on the train usually stops, thus making access even easier.

My train came trundling into view and I stuck out my arm to signal it to stop as required at request stops. The train driver sounded a note on his horn to indicate he had seen me. I was the only person waiting to get on and no one got off. I had my own personal stop.

We crossed back from Anglesey to mainland Wales on the Britannia bridge. When it was first built in 1846 it allowed, for the first time, trains to run to Holyhead and thus make ferry connections to Ireland. However, it was a complex project as the admiralty insisted that there was enough clearance under it for a fully rigged man-of-war. Which I can only assume is a type of boat. It was a similar construction to the bridge at Conway, with the trains running inside a tunnel on the bridge.

In 1970 the bridge suffered a devasting fire, caused by boys playing in the tunnels on the bridge dropping a lit flaming torch. The fire spread from one side to the other, with the fire brigade finding access difficult. When the bridge was assessed it was found to be so severely damaged that repair was not possible. They set about building a new one.

It took till 1972 before trains were running across the new bridge, but even then, the work was not complete. They carried on building and by 1980 there was a top deck added and the A55 runs across the same bridge on top of the trains.

Guarding the entrance to the original bridge were four stone lions. One each side of the track, two at each end of the bridge. These survived the fire and still stand guard to this day. They can be seen from trains fairly easily but cannot be seen from the A55.

The train joins the branches from Llandudno and Blaenau Ffestiniog at Llandudno Junction. It then gives sea views through Colwyn Bay and does not venture far inland through to Rhyl and Prestatyn. Back into England and Shotton station then Chester. With remarkable foresight the Romans even built a railway bridge into the city walls.

The train reverses at Chester and it is back past the racecourse. It is called The Roodee and is recognised by The Guinness Book Of World Records as the oldest racecourse still in use. It is also thought that it is the smallest, but there appears to be some doubt about that, although no one seems to be sure where from.

We then veer off the mainline and head to Wrexham. My penultimate station.

W

The train arrived at Wrexham General railway station. This used to be two stations until the mid-1980s, when what was Wrexham Exchange became Wrexham General platform 4.

Platform 4 still has it own entrance, it is just also connected to platforms 1, 2 and 3 by a footbridge too now. The word 'General' in a station name was used by the GWR to differentiate their main station from their competitors' stations. As the 'Big Four' gave way to British Rail such things were no longer required, and along with the Beeching cuts of the 1960s doing away with many duplicate stations, Wrexham remains the only station with General in its title.

Just a short stroll, or train ride from Platform 4, away is Wrexham Central. As the name implies it is more central. But it has less trains. As Wrexham General is not that far away either it is the more popular of the two stations. However, Wrexham central is in the middle of a retail park so very handy for the shops. The station was actually relocated by 250meters when they built the shops. It is now sitting between ASDA and Argos.

Wrexham sits in Wales, but it really could not be closer, geographically, to England. It is the largest town in North Wales. It has tried three times to become a city, but it is a case of always the bridesmaid and never the bride. It does not give up though and even has a Cathedral. It is called 'Our Lady of Sorrows' which isn't a happy title however you look at it and the marketing team may need to have a rethink on that if they want to draw in the crowds. The Catholic church may have joy, peace and eternal life, but no one seems to have told the Church naming committee that. Not unsurprisingly the locals call it 'St Marys Cathedral'.

The National Trust have a property, Erdigg Hall, just two miles from Wrexham, when I was a small boy, I remember we came to visit it, my Mum, Sister and I. I really cannot have been very old at all. I remember nothing of the place except for the very long walk to get there. The exceedingly long walk indeed. It may have been only two miles, but when you are only little it is a really long way. Of course, like all stately homes, arriving at the entrance is only the start, there is still a long entrance drive to go.

I did not intend to repeat the experience today. Another one I am keen not to repeat is that when we did get back to Wrexham, we saw the station sign and waited on a bench in the town waiting till closer to the train time before heading to the station. When we did head over, we found ourselves at the wrong Wrexham station! There followed a mad dash across the town.

Today I would stay in the town and keep my bearings. There is a catchily titled 'Wrexham County Borough Museum', which is free to go in, so I went in. It is everything you expect of a council museum. But it did have an excellent coffee shop which they described as "featuring some of the area's best food."

Ensuring I was headed to the correct station, I set off. Just one more station to go. It was, alas, going to require a change of train. But the end was in sight.

Back at Wrexham General I boarded a train for Shrewsbury and changed there onto a Manchester train. On the way we passed through Yorton. It could have been a contender, but as far as I can make out, the only thing at Yorton is the station. And with a train every two hours it is a long time to kill.

At Manchester I change trains again. The final train to my final station. York, here I come.

X

There is nowhere on Britain's rail network that starts with an X. I did not feel a 'crossing' was worthy of a visit just because it can, sometimes, be represented by a x on a map. It is not its full name.

Neither did a station such as Crossflatts, Crosshill or the wonderfully named Crossmyloof fit the bill. They start with X no more than Penzance starts with B.

I went straight to Y without an X. I carried on, on my way to York.

Y

York station is wonderful. The current building opened in 1877, although an original station (in a different location) had opened in 1839. It was found to be too small and outside of the city walls. In 1841 a new station was built inside the city walls. But it required trains from the North to reverse to reach London, which was a bit tiresome, so the current station was built, once again outside the city walls.

To celebrate my final station, Cath and the children joined me for a day out. To kick off the day as tourists we got the open-top sightseeing bus from outside the station. Our plan was cunningly simple, stay on the bus till we saw an attraction we fancied then get off.

We made it as far as the Castle museum. The castle museum is on the former site of York castle, although nothing remains of that now. The building is instead the former debtor's prison. Although it is built using stones from the castle ruins. It was very interesting and informative. It was the first place in Britain to build a reconstruction of a Victorian street.

Back outside, and Clifford's Tower is an original keep to the castle. Although only the outer walls survive, the floors, roof and central tower were all destroyed in an explosion in 1684. There are a lot of steps up to it, so we sent smallest child up to have a look whilst we waited at the bottom.

We waited for the open-top bus to come round and hopped back on.

We went down to the river and had a picnic. We strolled down the river side to the next bus stop and hopped back on the bus to York Minster. It was rather ambitiously priced at nearly £12 each to get in, so we did not bother. The National Trust have a property opposite and the garden is free to enter, so we went there instead. We got an ice cream then back on the bus.

We stayed on to the railway station again and got off to visit the National Railway Museum. This houses the national collection of railway memorabilia and is free to enter. It is home to The Mallard, the steam locomotive with the world speed record at 126mph. It is also home of the Flying Scotsman, although this isn't a static exhibit and it was off pulling a train when we were there; although we could still buy any number of souvenirs so we could remember having not seen it.

They also have Queen Victoria's Royal train, a palace on wheels. Just because she was not at home did not mean she did not have luxury. You can say what you like about the woman, but she knew how to travel in style.

We were going to grab something to eat, but the prices put us off, so we headed back to the station. There we found a Burger King. It may lack nutritional sustenance, unless you eat the lettuce leaf, but it is fast food. Except it was not. The service was so slow we would have missed our train had the train not been delayed. Maybe they factor in people buying fast food at York station.

Eventually, with food in hand, we made it onto the platform to join the swarming throngs waiting. The train was advertised as being six coaches long, it arrived fairly full already and the platform full of people squashed their way on. We were lucky and managed to get seats.

Then the guard announced that only the front three coaches would be leaving, so everyone in the rear three coaches would have to get off and get in the front three coaches. Everyone sat for a moment working out where they had boarded the train. We were in luck; we had got on the front three. The movement of people and detaching of the coaches only took forty minutes.

With six coaches of passengers now in three coaches, we set off a mere hour late. The train running an hour behind, and on time, virtually empty. I saw it when it overtook us in Leeds.

And thus, it was that I completed twenty-four stations, in alphabetical order. But it was not quite the end of the journey.

Z

I travelled to Burton Joyce station in Nottinghamshire. Who the Joyce is in the town name, I know not. Although Burton is a corruption of Bertune, another name for Hillfort. Archaeological digs have found evidence the town was in existence in the Mesolithic period. This place is old.

However, my interest is not in Burton Joyce, so I catch a bus. It is not a long ride and it drops me on the edge of town, on the A612 where it becomes a dual carriageway.

I spot the gap in the fence I am looking for. There are houses opposite, but this side of the road is farmland. The path is well worn and only accessible by foot. But, crucially if you are a lawyer, it is not a footpath. I guess it could be a foot path, but most certainly it is not a footpath.

I walk along the foot path till it meets the railway, here is my journeys end. The crossing of the railway line in front of me is Zulus crossing. The only place on Britain's rail network to start with Z.

It is also not a pedestrian crossing. This is why it is so important to the lawyers that no footpath leads to it. It is, officially, a 'User Worked Crossing.' This means a farmer can arrive in a farm vehicle and use the phone to ask the signalman for permission to cross. It gives access to his fields either side of the railway. There is no path the other side as there is a track wide enough for tractors, and whatever else farmers use, to get down. This side it just goes straight into the field. But there remains this strip of land down the side, that is not a footpath.

The Ramblers Association have campaigned for it to be made a footpath and for the crossing to be made a pedestrian crossing. But to no avail. Two public enquiries have been held and both found in favour of Network Rail. Not that I mind, the fact the crossing is here at all and named Zulus is enough for me. I take one last look at the only railway place in Britain to start with a Z and head home a happy man. My mission is complete.

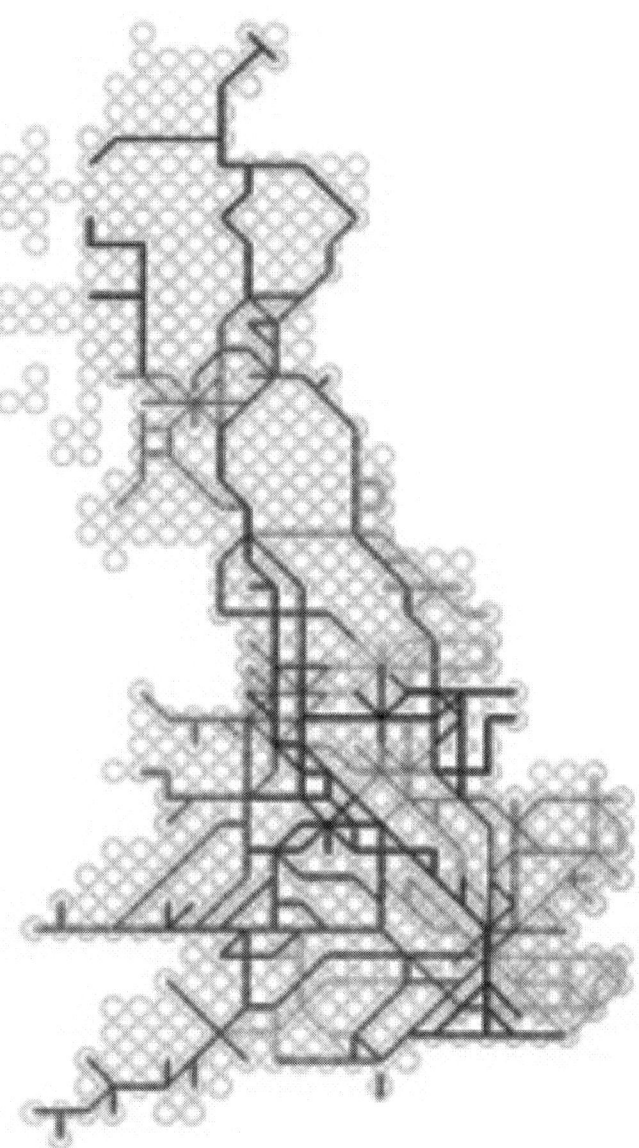

ACKNOWLEDGEMENT

My thanks must go to all the railway staff, without whom the journey would simply not have been possible. And esspecially those who could add knowledge and insight as I travelled. Working on Britains railways isn't just a job, it is a passion.

Harry worked tirelessly at producing the illustritive maps in this book that I trust you found helpful. He is to be thanked for that.

Martha responded to the call everytime I unwittingly did something stupid on the computer, be it changing font midway through a sentence or getting my typing to turn into pacman and gobble up all the previous test as I typed. She sorted it out each time without loosing paitence.

To Kristyan for the inspiration of the journey and the original idea. Even if he did not join me on this journey. I will make a train-spotter of him one day. In fairness, we did travel the Night Riviera sleeper together on a seperate ocassion as research. Thankfully Neil didn't remember us when I returned. Or if he did, he didn't let on.

To Catherine for continually checking and proofreading, as well as joining me on my travels at times. Her knowledge of English is far greater than this book shows. All errors remain, of course, mine and mine alone.

Finally, thanks to you, the reader. A book is nothing without someone to read it. Thank you.

ABOUT THE AUTHOR

Andy Keen

Andy was born in Rugby, the youngest of four children, to a Methodist minister. Their Father died of a heart attack six months later. The family then moved to Cheshire. He was educated at the Methodist Kingswood school in Bath. Andy's brother  died when he was 28. Andy had a heart attack and quintuple by-pass in December 2013 whilst living and working in Devon. Andy has three children and now lives and works in Staffordshire. Andy is marrying Cath in Spring 2021. Both Cath and Andy are active members of Rising Brook Community Church in Stafford.

BOOKS BY THIS AUTHOR

Heart And Souls

At just 43 Andy ended up in hospital after he had a heart attack. This book recounts the story of the heart attack, the heart bypass operation, and the exercise to recovery. Told in Andy's unique witty way, who would have thought a heart attack and recovery could be so funny.

Coconuts And Ice Cream

Most people don't travel anywhere via Australia, but Andy did. The Solomon Islands lie in the South Pacific, the villages do not have electricity but have rice and sweet potato in abundance. Everywhere is a canoe ride away. There are creatures that can injury you and cause you pain. Andy battles it all, and still talks in Church meetings each night.

Being part of the party that officially opened the 'Spotlight on Solomons' youth centre, he got to wear flower garlands and 'attacked' by warriors.

Andy even attended Synod, when he wasn't being ill. Learned some Pijin. And bought ice cream when he could.

In return the Solomon Islanders showed him just some of the hundred uses they have for the coconut.

Printed in Great Britain
by Amazon

50339734R00070